THE SYRIAC VERSION OF
THE WISDOM OF BEN SIRA COMPARED
TO THE GREEK AND HEBREW MATERIALS

SOCIETY
OF BIBLICAL
LITERATURE

DISSERTATION SERIES
J. J. M. Roberts, Old Testament Editor
Charles Talbert, New Testament Editor

Number 107
THE SYRIAC VERSION OF THE WISDOM OF BEN SIRA
COMPARED TO THE GREEK AND HEBREW MATERIALS

by
Milward Douglas Nelson

Milward Douglas Nelson

THE SYRIAC VERSION OF
THE WISDOM OF BEN SIRA
COMPARED TO THE GREEK
AND HEBREW MATERIALS

Scholars Press
Atlanta, Georgia

THE SYRIAC VERSION OF
THE WISDOM OF BEN SIRA COMPARED
TO THE GREEK AND HEBREW MATERIALS

Milward Douglas Nelson

Ph.D., 1981
University of California, Los Angeles

Advisor:
Stanislav Segert

© 1988
Society of Biblical Literature

Library of Congress Cataloging-in-Publication Data

Nelson, Milward Douglas, 1942–
   The Syriac version of the Wisdom of Ben Sira
compared to the Greek and Hebrew materials.

   (Dissertation series ; no. 107)
   Originally presented as the author's thesis
(Ph. D.)–University of California, Los Angeles, 1981.
   Bibliography: p.
   1. Bible. O.T. Apocrypha. Ecclesiasticus.
Syriac–Versions. 2. Bible. O.T. Apocrypha.
Ecclesiasticus–Sources. 3. Bible. O.T. Apocrypha.
Ecclesiasticus–Comparative studies. I. Title.
II. Series: Dissertation series (Society of Biblical
Literature) ; no. 107.
BS1765.5.S96N45   1988   229'.4043   87-28674

ISBN 1-55540-193-7 (alk. paper)
ISBN 1-55540-194-5 (pbk. : alk. paper)

Printed in the United States of America

Table of Contents

Acknowledgments

This dissertation is dedicated to my children, Marydawn and Michael Nelson, for being mine and for being so patient.

I also acknowledge the life-long support of my parents, my brothers, and my sister of my desires for learning and teaching. This is a small tribute to their loyalty.

I likewise acknowledge with gratitude my great teacher and patient friend, Prof. Dr. Stanislav Segert of the Department of Near Eastern Languages and Cultures, University of California, Los Angeles.

Abbreviations

A	Cairo Ms. A of Ben Sira
ATR	*Anglican Theological Review*
B	Cairo Ms. B of Ben Sira. See III. B.
Bm	Margin of Cairo Ms. B of Ben Sira. See III. B.
BASOR	*Bulletin of the American Schools of Oriental Research*
Bib	*Biblica*
C	Cairo Ms. C of Ben Sira
CBQ	*Catholic Biblical Quarterly*
D	Cairo Ms. D of Ben Sira
E	Cairo Ms. E of Ben Sira
ET	*Expository Times*
GI	Greek version of Ben Sira done by the grandson. See III. B.
GII	Later Greek version of Ben Sira. Codex 248 and related materials.
HTR	*Harvard Theological Review*
HUCA	*Hebrew Union College Annual*
JBL	*Journal of Biblical Literature*
JQR	*Jewish Quarterly Review*
K-B	Koehler & Baumgartner, *Lexicon in Veteris Testamenti Libros*
LXX	Septuagint
M	Masada Ms. of Ben Sira. See III. B.
RB	*Revue Biblique*
REJ	*Revue des Études Juives*
RQ	*Revue de Qumran*
Sm	Syriac Ms. of Ben Sira, Mosul edition. See III. B.
SL	Lagarde Syriac Ms. of Ben Sira, Vattioni edition. See III. B.
VT	*Vetus Testamentum*
Y	Yadin's edition of Ms. M. See III. B.
ZAW	*Zeitschrift für die Alttestamentliche Wissenschaft*
ZDMG	*Zeitschrift der deutschen morgenländischen Gesellschaft*
ZKT	*Zeitschrift für Katholische Theologie*
ZNW	*Zeitschrift für die neutestamentliche Wissenschaft*

1
History of Discoveries and Studies

A. THE WISDOM OF BEN SIRA: AUTHOR, PROVENANCE, AND DATE

Author and Title

The author of *Ecclesiasticus*[1] is called in Greek Ἰησοῦς υἱὸς Σιραχ Ελεαζαρ ὁ Ἱεροσολυμίτης (50:27). The title of the book is Σοφία Ἰησοῦ Υἱοῦ Σιραχ.[2]

In Hebrew the author's name is given as שמעון בן ישוע בן אלעזר בן סירא (50:27) or שמעון בן ישוע "who is called" בן סירא (51:30), and the title of the book as חכמת שמעון בן ישוע בן אלעזר בן סירא (51:30).

Syriac gives *ptgmwhy dyšw' br šm'wn* "who is called" *br 'syr'* (50:30, Vattioni), "the words (text) of Jesus Son of Shemon, who is called son of Asira."[3]

There is, as one can see, some confusion or conflation in the name as given in these sources.[4] If it is accepted that the name Simon has intruded into the Hebrew text at 50:27 and 51:30 on the basis of 50:1 or for some other reason, then the Greek name can be explained as a transposition of "son of Elazar" and "son of Sira." The Syriac has reversed "Simon son of Jesus" to read "Jesus son of Simon."

Thus we have the name of the author: "Jesus, son of Elazar, son of Sira."

Provenance and Date

Ben Sira wrote his book of Wisdom around 190 B.C. in Jerusalem. 50:1 refers to the high priest Simon, probably Simon II of the time of Ptolemy V and Antiochus III.[5] This Simon died in approximately 195 B.C. and was succeeded to the high priesthood by his son Onias III. This Onias was deposed by

---

[1] Latin, from ἐκκλησιαστικός. The title in codex 248 is Ἐκκλησιαστικός Σοφία Ἰησοῦ υἱοῦ Σιραχ. Vattioni: 1968, p. xi.

[2] See Ziegler: 1965, p. 127, for variants and alternatives.

[3] The Mosul edition, *Biblia Sacra*, adds *hkmt' dyšw' br šm'wn* "who is" *br syr'* (51:38), representing all the Hebrew.

[4] See Smend: 1906, II, pp. 492f; Vattioni: 1968, pp. x–xvii.

[5] A. H. Forster: 1959, pp. 1–9, refers to the several candidates for Simon and Euergetes and their bearing on the date of Ben Sira; R. Marcus identifies the Simon of Ben Sira 50:1 as Simon II of ca. 200 B.C., *Josephus* VII, pp. 732–736; Vattioni: 1968, p. xiv.

Antiochus Epiphanes (175–164) and by 171 Menelaus, not of Zadokite descent, was high priest. Since the *Wisdom of Ben Sira* does not mention these events, the book was most likely completed between 195 and 175 B.C., after Simon II but before Antiochus Epiphanes.[6]

The grandson of Ben Sira states that he "came to Egypt in the thirty-eighth year of the reign of Euergetes" (Prologue, 25) and that after a period of time he translated the *Wisdom of Ben Sira* into Greek. The Euergetes in question here is Ptolemy VII Euergetes II Physcon (170–117 B.C.), which would place the arrival of the grandson in Egypt at 132 B.C. The grandson implies that he had been in Egypt for a time before completing his translation; thus it can be dated somewhere between 120 B.C. and 117 B.C. (the death of Euergetes) or shortly thereafter. This information again would place the date of the original composition of Ben Sira around 190 or 180 B.C.,[7] allowing two generations of time.

B. THE HEBREW MANUSCRIPTS:
THEIR DISCOVERY AND PUBLICATION

The Cairo Manuscripts of Ben Sira

Beginning in 1896 two-thirds of Ben Sira in Hebrew had been discovered among the manuscripts of the Cairo Geniza.[8] The book had not been known in Hebrew for several centuries. In fact, there are no references to this book in Hebrew after Saadia in the tenth century, though it had been well-known in Hebrew before that time.[9]

The Hebrew manuscripts from the Cairo Geniza date from the eleventh and twelfth centuries. "The following is a brief summary of the contents and publication of the five manuscripts, A–E.

To 1900[10]

The initial identification of fragments in Hebrew from the Cairo Geniza as parts of the book of Ben Sira was done by S. Schecter of Cambridge University in 1896. Between 1896 and 1900, additional fragments were identified until 1056 distichs were known, as compared to 1616 in the Greek version.

---

[6] Vattioni, 200–170 B.C., ibid., pp. xvii–xviii.

[7] Eissfeldt: 1965, p. 597.

[8] Kahle: 1959, pp. 3ff.

[9] Quotations of Ben Sira in Talmudic and other rabbinical sources: Smend: 1906, II, pp. xlvi–lvi (esp. xliii–li); Vattioni: 1968 prints many of the rabbinic quotes; cf. L. Ginzberg: 1906, p. 615 and Cowley and Neubauer: 1897, pp. xix–xxx.

[10] Initial publications of Mss. A–D: Adler: 1899–1900, pp. 466–480. Cowley and Neubauer: 1897; Cowley and Neubauer: 1901. Gaster: 1899–1900, pp. 688–702. Lévi: 1898, 1901; Lévi: 1900; Lévi: 1904. Margoliouth: 1899–1900, pp. 1–33. Peters: 1902. Schechter: 1896, pp. 1–15; Schechter: 1897–1898, pp. 197–206; Schechter: 1899–1900, pp. 456–465. Schechter and Taylor: 1899. Smend: 1906, I. Strack: 1903.

A 2:18a (?); 3:66-7:29a; 11:34b-16:26a/ 7:29-12:1
   23:16, 17 inserted after 12:14; 27:5, 6 after 6:22.
   (six leaves, 11th century)

B 30:11-31:11; 32:1b-33:3; 35:11-36:26; 37:27-38:27b; 49:12c-end/
   39:15c-40:8/ 40:9-49:11.
   (19 leaves, 12th century)
   Each verse is on a separate line, divided into two hemistichs; thus
   each page is divided into two columns.

C 4:23b, 30, 31; 5:4-7c, 9-13; 36:24a/ 6:18b, 19, 28, 35; 7:1, 2, 4, 6ab,
   17, 20, 21, 23-25/ 18:31b-19:2a; 20:5-7; 37:19, 22, 24, 26; 20:13/
   25:8, 13, 17-24; 26:1, 2.
   (four leaves, before 11th century)

D 36:29-38:1a
   (one leaf, eleventh century)

1931[11]

In 1931 J. Marcus published a new leaf of Ben Sira. This leaf, MS Adler
3597 of the Jewish Theological Seminary of America, was designated as MS E
and added 34 new distichs to the known Hebrew of Ben Sira.

E 32:16-22; 33:1; 32:24; 33:2, 4, 5-32; 34:1
   Like B, each verse is on a separate line, divided into two
   hemistichs.

1958, 1960[12]

More leaves of manuscripts B and C were identified and published by J.
Schirman in 1958 and 1960. Among the 81 distichs published were 7½ previously
unknown in Hebrew. This brought the total to 1098 distichs in Hebrew, 68% of
the 1616 known from Greek.

B 10:9-20, 22-24; 7:21a; 10:25-31; 11:1-10; 15:1-16:7
   (two leaves)

C 3:14-18, 21, 22; 41:16; 4:21; 20:22-23; 26:2b-3, 13, 15-17; 36:27-31.
   (two leaves)
   Seven and one-half distichs previously unknown: 20:22-33;
   26:2b-3, 13, 13-17.

[11] Publications after the discovery of 1931: Lévi: 1932. Marcus: 1931; Marcus: 1930-31.
[12] Publication of the discovery of 1958: DiLella: 1964, pp. 153-167. Schirmann:
1957-1958, pp. 440-443; Schirmann: 1959-1960, pp. 125-134. Segal: 1958. Includes the first
of Schirmann's publications.

For some time there was skepticism regarding the authenticity and reliability of these manuscripts, due to considerable variation among them and to some inexplicable marginal notations. Now, however, there is general consensus that the Geniza manuscripts represent the original Hebrew version, though in a corrupted form, and perhaps traceable as far back as Qumran.[13]

The Qumran Fragments of Ben Sira

Among the Qumran scrolls have been identified fragments of the Wisdom of Ben Sira in Hebrew. In 1956f two fragments from Cave 2 were found to be parts of Ben Sira Chapter 6, and in 1965 parts of Chapter 51 from Cave 11 were published.

2Q 18[14]

> 6:14, 15 (or 1:19–20); 6:20–31
> (second half of first century)
> Arranged like B and E, with each verse on a separate line and divided into hemistichs. 6:20–31 is practically the same text as MS A.

11Q Ps^a[15]

> 51:13–20,30b
> (first half of first century)

The Masada Manuscript of Ben Sira[16]

In 1964 a spectacular discovery of a large portion of Ben Sira in Hebrew was made during the excavations of Y. Yadin at Masada. The Hebrew fragment consists of 39:27–44:17 and dates from the early first century B.C.

This completes the list of Hebrew manuscripts and fragments of Ben Sira. After a brief consideration of the Greek and Syriac versions, we will present a history of the scholarly study of these materials. The following is a synopsis of the contents of the book now available in Hebrew:

Verses	Manuscripts
1:19,20 (?)	2Q18 (Vattioni, p. 7)
2:18a (?)	A (The Book of Ben Sira, p. 3)

---

[13] See below, section E, "History of the Study of Ben Sira."
[14] Baillet, Milik, deVaux: 1962, pp. 75–77. Baillet: 1956, p. 54. Segal: 1964, pp. 243ff.
[15] Sanders 1965, pp. 79–85. See Delcor: 1968, pp. 27–47 for corrections.
[16] Yadin: 1965, pp. 1–45. Baumgarten: 1968, pp. 323–327. Milik: 1966, pp. 425ff. Skehan: 1966, pp. 260–262. Strugnell: 1969/70, pp. 109–119. Eck: 1969, pp. 282–289. Dates the fall of Masada in 74 A.D. on the basis of recently discovered coins.

3:6b–16:26a	A,B,C,2Q18
18:31b–19:2a,3b	C
20:4,5,6,7,13,22,23	B,C
23:16b	A
25:8,13,17–24	C
26:1–3,13,15–17	C
27:5,6,16 (?)	A,B (27:16?) (Vattioni, p. 145)
30:11–34:1	B,E
35:9–38:27	B,C
36:29–38:1	D
39:15c–51:30	B,C (41:15), M, 11QPsa

C. THE GREEK VERSION

Greek I and II

There is now general agreement that the Greek version exists in at least two forms: Greek I and Greek II. Greek I is the version of Ben Sira's grandson and Greek II is a later version probably based on a different form of the Hebrew text.[17]

Before Ziegler, most scholars divided the Greek witnesses into two groups: (1) BSA (followed in Aldine and Sixtine editions); and (2) sc; group containing cursive 248; mostly *Vetus Latina*, Syriac, Syrohexapla, and Complutensian Polyglot.[18] And the order of transmission of Ben Sira was reconstructed as follows:[19]

(1) Hebrew original;
(2) Greek version of the grandson (Gr. I), (group 1);
(3) Revised Hebrew text;
(4) Greek version of the Hebrew revision (Gr. II), primarily represented in cursive 248 (group 2).[20]

Ziegler concurs that Greek I is contained in the major uncials BSACV and the cursives which follow them. However, he argues that Greek II is not an independent new translation which we now have in a complete form. Instead, it was affected by Greek I and now only parts of it can be reconstructed from variant readings in Greek cursives, especially codex 248, *Vetus Latina*, quotations in Clement of Alexandria, Chrysostom and some Biblical florilegia.[21]

[17] See Ziegler: 1965 for detailed information on manuscripts (pp. 7–13), translations (13–37), quotations (37–40) and printed editions (40–53) of the Greek version of Ben Sira; also, Vattioni: 1968, p. xxiv, notes 47, 48, 49.

[18] See Jellicoe: 1968, p. 308.

[19] W. O. E. Oesterley: 1935, pp. 249–51.

[20] Edited by J. H. A. Hart: 1909.

[21] Ziegler: 1965, pp. 37–39, 75ff.

Ziegler also carefully dstinguishes Hexaplaric and Lucianic recensions of the Greek of Ben Sira,[22] insisting that these recensions provide evidence of the additions to Ben Sira — evidence of the Hebrew *Vorlage* to Greek II.

Greek I and II are thus derived from different Hebrew *Vorlagen;* the manuscripts from Cairo often preserve both. For example, Ziegler says:

> At the same time, the new text [Heb. MSB, 15:1–16:7] shows that it often is not the *Vorlage* of the translation of the grandson (Gr. I), but of the later so-called second translation (Gr. II).[23]

He then presents this example:

15:16   *tšlḥ* (B) = ἐκτενεῖς (Gr. I)
            šlḥ (A) = ἐκτεινον (Gr. II)

Rearrangement of the Text

A transposition of two leaves in the Hebrew *Vorlage* of the Greek version has caused a rearrangement of parts of chapters 33–36 in the Greek version.[24] Ziegler has preserved the Greek order in his edition but has put the numbers in parentheses to clarify their relationship to the other versions.[25]

Hebrew/Syriac/ *Vetus Latina*/Armenian		Greek Numbering	Greek Order
30:25–40	=	33:16b–33	30:27
31	=	34	31
32	=	35	32
33:1–13a	=	36:1–13a	33:1–16a
33:13b	=	30:7	33:16b–33
34	=	31	34
35	=	32	35
36:1–16a	=	33:1–16a	36:1–13a
36:16b	=	36:16b	

D. THE SYRIAC VERSION[26]

The Syriac Version of Ben Sira was translated from a Hebrew original and not from Greek, though it does represent a later form of the Hebrew somewhat expanded. Ziegler observes, "Syr geht nicht auf G, sondern auf H zuruck;

---

[22] Ziegler: 1959, pp. 210–229; 1965, pp. 57–80.
[23] Ziegler 1965, p. 83. Translation and parenthesis mine.
[24] H. B. Swete: 1907, 2, pp. vi–vii.
[25] Ziegler: 1965, pp. 279–291.
[26] See below, Chapter II "The Syriac Versions, Manuscripts and Editions of the Old Testament and the Place of Ben Sira in Them" for bibliography and publications of the Syriac materials.

deshalb wird Syr nur gelegentlich Zitiert."[27] A number of scholars had made this conjecture even before the discovery of the Cairo Hebrew manuscripts, but the theory was not generally accepted until after those events.[28]

Most probably this version was done from a Hebrew text different from the one used by the grandson (Gr. I) but also guided by a Greek version which contained many Greek II readings. It preserves the correct order of chapters 33-36, which are inverted in Greek I, and does not contain the grandson's prologue. The Syriac contains some material unique to itself (37 distichs) and some which agrees with the Greek II but departs from the Hebrew (35 distichs).[29]

The origin, transmission and nature of the Syriac Version will be considered more fully in subsequent Chapters II and V.

E. HISTORY OF THE STUDY OF BEN SIRA[30]

The original editors of the Cairo Geniza fragments—Schechter and Taylor, and later Marcus and Schirmann—defend their authenticity in spite of some peculiar glosses and marginal notes and the complicated relationship of the manuscripts to one another.[31] These scholars were supported in their judgment by many others, such as Nöldeke, Toy, Smend, Fuchs, Peters, Lagarde, Box and Oesterley, and Segal. This consensus was achieved by 1915 and held until nearly 1940.

Segal

Segal, in a position somewhat typical of the others, states the condition and evaluation of the witnesses to Ben Sira as of 1934:

---

[27] Ziegler: 1965, p. 31; Rüger: 1970¹, pp. 112ff: Originally separate forms of the Hebrew text were somewhat amalgamated at later date; Syriac translated one form and Greek the other.

[28] Cf. Smend: 1906, II, pp. cxxvi-cxxxvii: Cornelius a Lapide (cf. J. Knabenbauer, *Commentarius in Ecclesiasticum, Cursus Scripturae Sacrae*, ed. Cornely et al., II 2,6, Parisiis, 1902); Benedict Bendtsen, *Specimen exercitationum criticarum in V. T. libros apocryphos* (Göttinger Dissertation, 1789) p. 16; A. Geiger, *ZDMG* XII, pp. 530ff; J. Perles, *Meletemata Peshitthoniana* (1859); Th. Nöldeke, *Alttestamentliche Literatur* (1868) p. 168; G. Bickell, *Zeitschrift fur Katholische Theologie*, 6 (1882) pp. 319ff; *Wiener Zeitschrift fur Kunde des Morgenlandes* VI (1892) pp. 87ff; A. Edersheim, *Ecclesiasticus. Apocrypha*, ed. by H. Wace, Vol. II (London, 1888).

[29] See below, Chapter V "Omissions, Additions and Alterations in the Syriac Version." Kahle: 1959, p. 269 says that agreements with the Hebrew text in the Peshitta belong to the oldest parts of the Peshitta and the influences of the LXX are due to Christian amendments to the Peshitta.

[30] This section is essentially a review of the research of DiLella: 1966 and additional literature since then.

[31] See Chapter 1, nn. 10-12 for literature.

The text of Ben Sira has come down to us in three recensions, viz., the Greek of the LXX and its daughter versions, the Syriac of the Peshitta, and the Hebrew fragments. Each of these recensions represents a different type of text which ultimately goes back to the primitive Hebrew text of the author. Of these only the Syriac may be said to be of a uniform character. All the extant Syriac Mss. exhibit with but slight variations one and the same text. The other two recensions represent a mixed type of text. The variations between certain groups of the Greek Mss. are often so far-reaching as to force us to subdivide the Greek recension into a main type, represented by the uncial Mss., and a sub-type, represented by the cursive cod. 248 and its associates, to which also belong the Latin and the Syro-Hexaplar versions. Likewise, the Hebrew Mss., where they overlap, often exhibit differences of an important character, e.g., Mss. B and D in ch. 37.16–38, 1; Mss. B and E . . . in ch. 32.16–33.2. To these must also be added the differences between the text of Mss. B and its marginal glosses.[32]

The relationship between these materials, again typical of the theories of other defenders of the authenticity of the Hebrew fragments, is presented by Segal in the following remark and chart:

The primitive Hebrew text of Ben Sira gave rise to four different Hebrew recensions, viz. (in their chronological order), the originals of Gr. I, of Gr. II, and of Syr., and the text of the Hebrew fragments. Of these only one may be said to be descended from an older recension, viz., Gr. II from Gr. I. All the others developed directly from the primitive text, but the later recensions, Syr. and Heb., have been influenced by the older recensions, Gr. I and Gr. II, and Syr. (in the case of Heb.).[33]

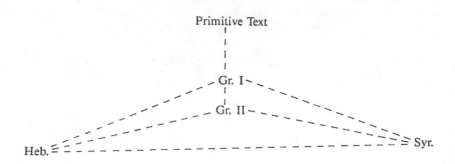

[32] M. H. Segal: 1934, p. 91.
[33] Ibid., pp. 148ff.

Rabbinic Quotations

Nestle and Levi. E. Nestle and I. Levi, during this early consensus period, held theories of general authenticity, but allowing for some retroversion from Syriac or Greek. Levi went through several changes of opinion between 1896 and 1904,[34] ultimately arguing that the Hebrew text of the Geniza fragments was essentially authentic but partly retroverted from Syriac.[35] According to Nestle, Hebrew Ms. C is partly retroverted from Greek and Ms. A partly from Syriac. Of this theory he says:

> Not even of C is it possible to say that it is a *simple retranslation* of G, for even in C there are passages which are at variance with G. On the other hand, it is equally impossible to maintain that H has preserved everywhere the original, independent of G and S. There are passages in H which cannot be explained in any other way than by supposition that they rest on a corrupt and glossed text, sometimes of G, sometimes of S.[36]

Early Opponents of the Consensus

D. S. Margoliouth's study of Ms. B led him to conclude that the Hebrew text was a retranslation from Persian and Syriac into Hebrew. The Persian version itself was made from Greek and the rendering from Persian and Syriac into Hebrew was done by a Persian-speaking Jew around 1000 A.D.[37]

G. Bickell in 1899 likewise rejected the authenticity of the Geniza Hebrew fragments. He argued on the basis of studies of Ben Sira 51:13–30 and 12:10–11 that the Hebrew manuscripts were translated from Syriac originals.[38]

Both Margoliouth and Bickell were refuted by the "consensus" scholars of the time.[39]

Revival of Opposition

For a twenty year period beginning around 1940, a number of scholars again advocated theories of total retroversion of the Geniza Hebrew from Greek or Syriac.

E. J. Goodspeed in 1939 stated in his introduction to the Apocrypha:

---

[34] See DiLella: 1966, pp. 25ff and notes.

[35] I. Lévi: 1904.

[36] E. Nestle: 1923, "Sirach (Book of)," *A Dictionary of the Bible,* 4, ed. by J. Hastings (New York: Scribners, 1923) p. 548.

[37] *The Origin of the "Original Hebrew" of Ecclesiasticus* (London-Oxford, 1899) pp. 19ff. Cited in DiLella: 1966, pp. 26ff.

[38] "Der hebraische Sirachtext eine Rückübersetzung," *Wiener Zeitschrift fur die Kunde des Morgenlandes* 13 (1899) pp. 251–256. Cited in DiLella: 1966, pp. 30ff.

[39] See DiLella: 1966, pp. 29 (nn. 28–35) and 31 (n. 39) for literature.

. . . the original Hebrew of this book no longer exists. The considerable Hebrew portions of Ecclesiasticus, amounting to about two-thirds of the whole, that have come to light in recent years in medieval manuscripts are probably retranslations of it from Greek back into its original tongue; nothing remains of the original Hebrew.[40]

And then in 1959 M. Hadas supported the same theory of retroversion from Greek.[41]

C. C. Torrey, following very disparaging remarks about the quality of the Hebrew of Ben Sira, suggests a retroversion of the book from Syriac:

> In and shortly after 1896 there came to light fragments of a Hebrew text of the book, the source of them being the geniza (storeroom) of a Cairo synagogue. Eventually they amounted to considerably more than half of the work. These fragments were then hailed, and are now commonly accepted, as surviving portions of the original Hebrew text. There is strong reason for questioning this verdict. It is possible to see back of the Greek version a powerful and original Hebrew text, the work of a master of the literary language. In the Cairo Hebrew this impression is not maintained. What we read in a multitude of passages is commonplace, flabby, and distinctly second rate. It is customary to excuse much of this as "late Hebrew." The trouble is not with the character of the language, however, but with the lack of literary taste and skill. It is exactly what would be expected of a well-equipped writer of (say) the eighth or ninth century who should undertake, without any profound study, to reproduce the text of Ecclesiasticus, basing his work mainly on the Syriac version.[42]

The book of Ben Sira was removed from the corpus of "Hebrew" literature in the time of Akiba and eventually disappeared.[43] According to Torrey the Geniza manuscripts which we now have were based on a Syriac version from the Middle Ages.[44] H. L. Ginsberg, in an article in which he reconstructs what he thinks is the original Hebrew of Ben Sira 12:10-14, suggests that the Geniza Hebrew fragments are based on Syriac, Syrohexapla, and some Biblical flourishes:

> 1. The Greek version of Ben Sira (G) is an about 90% literal rendering of a smooth, pleasing Hebrew.
> 2. The Peshitta (S) of this Book is clearly a very free rendering of a Hebrew text which diverged but little from that which served G as archetype.
> 3. The Genizah Hebrew text (H) is composed in an idiom which (a) is for the most part hideous, (b) is rarely presupposed by G, (c) for the most part alternates between execrably literal reproduction of S and substitution of biblical (or other) flourishes which only vaguely suggest the general of S. In addition to S, the Syrohexaplar Version (Sh) was occasionally consulted by the producer or producers of H.[45]

40 1939, p. 25.
41 1959, p. 222.
42 1945, p. 97.
43 C. C. Torrey: 1950, pp. 585–602.
44 Ibid., pp. 601f.
45 1955, p. 93.

Duesberg and Auvray base their translation of Ben Sira on the Greek version. Their view is that the Geniza Hebrew is of a very late recension, not reliable, and many passages are retranslations from Greek.[46]

Thus, the opposition to the authenticity of the Hebrew of Ben Sira from the Cairo Geniza rose again with considerable force in the period ca. 1940–1960. The opponents adhered to theories of retroversion from Greek (Goodspeed, Hadas, Duesberg and Auvray or Syriac (Torrey, Ginsberg).

Authenticity and Partial Retroversion: DiLella

In 1962 and 1963 Alexander DiLella completed a doctoral dissertation and published two articles on the Hebrew text of Sirach.[47] These works were followed in 1966 by the publication of his book, *The Hebrew Text of Sirach. A Text-Critical and Historical Study*, which provides a thorough survey of opinion regarding the Hebrew manuscripts from Cairo, a defense of the authenticity of the manuscripts, and his own theory of "partial retroversion" from Syriac.[48] I will present here a brief review of his chief arguments.

Text-critical proofs of authenticity

1. Biblical citations in the Geniza text which agree with the *Vorlage* of the LXX instead of the MT indicate that the Geniza text antedates 132 A.D. (when the consonantal text was fixed), or perhaps even 68 A.D. (Qumran cave IV shows that a *Vorlage* of the LXX was in use then). There are two such citations: 46:19c (quoting 1 Sam 12:3) and 31:2b (Is 38:17). (DiLella, pp 47–49)
2. The order of chapters in the Geniza text shows that it predates the Greek whose displacement of chapters was complete by the end of the third or in the fourth century A.D. (Chapters 30–36 are rearranged in all Greek Mss. and daughter translations, except *Vetus Latina*, Armenian, and Slavonic). Syriac, Latin and another Armenian tradition preserve the original order. Three passages — 30:24, 25; 33:16, 17; 36:13ab — show that Geniza Hebrew forms base for Syriac and Greek. Geniza Hebrew text base predates both Greek and Syriac. (DiLella, pp 49–55)
3. Selected passages from each of the five manuscripts show upon comparison with Syriac and Greek that the Geniza Hebrew is the original: 7:20, 25; 10:19; 15:19; 32:20; 36:31; 37:1, 2, 6. (DiLella, pp 55–77)

---

[46] Duesberg and Auvray: 1953, p. 19. The edition of 1958 adds Syriac on p. 19, "Enfin la qualite meme de la langue et certaines comparisons avec les versions grecque *et syria-que* ont fait parler, pour certain fragments du moins, d'une retraduction." Cf. Louis F. Hartman: 1961, pp. 443–451 for a review of the two editions (1953, 1958).
[47] 1962¹, 1962², 1963.
[48] See Chapter 1, n. 30.

Historical proofs of authenticity

1. Qumran cave II has produced two fragments containing portions of Ben Sira: 6:14–15 (or 1:19–20) and 6:20–31. The text of the latter passage is virtually identical to Ms. A and has the same stichometric arrangement as Mss. B and E. (DiLella, pp 78–81)

2. To the question, "How did Medieval Jews come by a text of Ben Sira in Hebrew and in stichometric arrangement?", DiLella answers that they found it in a cave near Jericho.

   a. A Syriac letter dating 796/797 A.D. from Timothy I (727/728–823 A.D.), Nestorian Patriarch of Selucia, to Sergius, Metropolitan of Elam, mentions a discovery of Hebrew manuscripts in a cave near Jericho. This cave was perhaps one of the Qumran caves[49] which contained among its preserved materials a copy of Ben Sira in Hebrew. (DiLella, pp 81–84)

   b. Three medieval scholars—Ja'qub al-Qirqisani (10th century A.D.), Shahrastani (1076–1153), and Atar al-Bakiya—refer to a Jewish sect, "Cave People," of pre- or early Christian times. These "Cave People" are to be identified with the Essenes from Qumran. Among their non-Biblical books was Ben Sira in Hebrew, which was found and copied by Jews ca. 800 A.D. (DiLella, pp 84–105)

Partial Retroversion from Syriac

The chief arguments used against the authenticity of the Geniza Hebrew texts of Ben Sira are that the Hebrew idiom is terrible and that there are many clear affinities to the Syriac. Even those who accept the authenticity of the Hebrew fragments claim evidence in the Geniza text for *two* recensions—the *Vorlage* to Greek (classical Hebrew) and the *Vorlage* to Syriac (late Hebrew);[50] in the doublets, the primitive text is from the Greek *Vorlage* and modernized doublets are from the Syriac *Vorlage*.

DiLella disagrees with both: the "terrible" Hebrew idiom and the doublets can be explained by "partial retroversion" from Syriac. (DiLella, pp 106f) Syriac was known among Jewish scholars at the time when the Cairo manuscripts were copied (9–12th centuries A.D.). (DiLella, pp 107f)

DiLella gives a number of examples of this "partial retroversion" from Syriac, which he insists is not widespread. (DiLella, pp 108–147) One example will suffice: 10:31cd is preserved in Heb. A and B, but not in Greek or Syriac. However, 31ab in Syriac—which is apparently a translation of Heb. 31ab—provides the form of the text from which Heb. 31cd was "retroverted."

---

[49] See Kahle: 1959, pp. 16ff; de Vaux: 1950, pp. 419ff.
[50] Including Ziegler: 1965 p. 83.

	Ms. B	Ms. A

Heb. 31c   המתכבד בדלותו בעשרו   [המתה]כבד בדלותו בעשרו
                       מתכבד יתר   מתכבד יתר

Heb. 31d   והנקלה בעשרו בדלותו   והנקלה בעשרו בדלותו
                       נקלה יתר   נקלה יותר

Syriac 31a (Walton) *dmtyqr bmsknwt'* (*bmsknwth*, Ambrosianus, Lagarde, Mosul) *b'wtrh ḥd km'*

Syriac 31b (Walton, Mosul) *bmsknwth b'wtrh ḥd km'* (Ambrosianus, Lagarde) *wdzlyl b'mtrh bmsknwth ḥd km'*

Heb. 31cd "He who is honored in his poverty is honored more in his wealth, and he who is lightly esteemed in his wealth is more lightly esteemed in his poverty."

Syriac 31cd "He who is honored in (his) poverty, in his wealth how much more? And he who is despised in his poverty, in his wealth how much more?"

Ms. A introduced this passage on the basis of 10:31ab in the Syriac and then it was copied by the scribe of Ms. B: Mishnaic style and vocabulary is found in the Hebrew addition (מתכבד; דלות for נכבד), which indicates that the addition (i.e., 10:31cd) was made at a late date; 10:31ab in the Syriac presents third person singular suffixes on "poverty" and "wealth"—these words and suffixes are also found in Hebrew 10:31cd. (DiLella, pp. 115 119)

Conclusion and Chronology

DiLella draws seven conclusions from his text-critical study:

1. Geniza Mss. are very near the original text of Ben Sira.
2. Retroversions from Syriac are few and surrounded by genuine material.
3. Greek, Syriac, and Old Latin are often corrupt and only the Geniza material is authentic.
4. Yet, the Geniza Mss. contain many corruptions.
5. "Partial retroversion" from Syriac explains much "hideous" and "late" Hebrew.
6. Retroversions from Syriac form a major part of the Geniza corruptions.
7. Opponents of the genuineness of the Geniza Hebrew cannot prove that the whole text of Ben Sira is based on Persian (Margoliouth), Greek (Goodspeed, Hadas), Syriac (Torrey, Bickell, Ginsberg), or Syrohexapla (Ginsberg). (DiLella, pp 148f)

He then presents the following chronology for Ben Sira from its beginning to the publication of the Cairo Geniza manuscripts:

1. Book written in Palestine, ca. 200–175 B.C.
2. Many copies were made and circulated. After 132 B.C. a Greek translation was made in Egypt. The Essenes at Qumran had a copy of the Hebrew.
3. At Jamnia, the rabbis suppress the book.
4. A Syriac version is made from a Hebrew (2nd–4th century A.D.) recension different from that at Qumran.
5. Hebrew survives to the time of Jerome (d. 420 A.D.).
6. Hebrew Ben Sira gone by mid-5th century A.D. Occasionally quoted by the rabbis from memory.
7. Ca. 800 A.D., Hebrew text found in cave near Jericho.
8. Qaraites who found the text make copies; some poorly preserved parts are translated into Hebrew from Syriac.
9. Qaraites and other Jews (eg. Saadia) use the Hebrew until 12th century when it is again suppressed. Hebrew copies disappear into the Genizas.
10. In 1896 ff (Mss. ABCD), 1931 (Ms. E), 1958 and 1960 (more of Mss. B and C), Hebrew Mss. of Ben Sira from Cairo Geniza are published. (DiLella, pp 150f)

Recent Study

The Masada Manuscript.[51] This Ms., dating from the first century B.C., gives testimony to the general faithfulness of Greek I and the Cairo Geniza Hebrew manuscripts, while at the same time showing how some changes have come about through corruption and paraphrasing. This is the status of the present evaluation of the manuscript by most scholars.

Yadin places the composition of the manuscript between 125–100 B.C. and 50–25 B.C., i.e., somewhere around 75 B.C., in a middle or Late Hasmonean script.[52] By comparing M, B text, B margin, G, and S, he draws these conclusions:

1. M basically confirms that the Geniza Mss. represent the original Hebrew, though corrupted by copyists' errors and other developments;
2. When B text and B margin differ, they represent two recensions which diverged from each other prior to the date of the Geniza Mss.;
3. B text is a more popular version, possibly influenced by that among the Qumran sect;
4. B text "Hebraized" Aramaic words or explained difficult words by more common Biblical words;
5. The text used by G is closest to M;
6. Syriac agrees with M much less than does G and is not so dependent on G.[53]

---

[51] See above, n. 16.
[52] Yadin: 1965, p. 4.
[53] Ibid., pp. 1, 4, 6, 9, 10, 11.

Thus M is closer to the original and is an archetype for several recensions, among which were those consulted by B text and B margin.[54]

Th. Middendorp in 1973 published a book, *Die Stellung Jesu Ben Sira Zwischen Judentum und Hellenismus,* in which he discussed the influence of Greek thought and education and the Hebrew Old Testaent on the work of Ben Sira.[55] In the central part of the book he makes some remarks on the Masada and Geniza manuscripts, and the Greek version that are appropriate here. First, he studied a number of passages regarding the "synonyms" between M, B, B marg. and G — i.e., those cases in which a similar idea is expressed in the various versions with different words. He concludes that where the differences are slight, they can be attributed to scribal error, but when another similar word is used, the change is due to failure in memory or intentional change.[56] The fact that these books were learned by rote allowed such alterations to take place.

From this study of synonyms he observes that G faithfully preserves its Vorlage, and that B and M often have a close relationship, perhaps the former deriving from the latter.[57] The primary explanation for the differences is not that the traditions are not genuine, but that changes occurred as a result of oral transmission.[58]

Secondly, Middendorp studies the relationship between M and G, and reaches these conclusions:

1. M, B, B marg., G have 57 passages in common and there are deviations among them in readings; M and G agree in 41 of the 57;
2. The *Vorlage* of G is not the original text; the failure of the strophic structure caused omission of half-lines and false version divisions;
3. G goes back faithfully to its Vorlage, except in those cases where G changes a word for clarification or is influenced by the Greek Bible;
4. B marg. usually coincides with M, but gives some variants which are not so valuable;
5. B is often worse than M and G; it has some omissions and its mistakes are of the memory type; when B and G agree (41:26–42:6; 43:30), M may nevertheless be original;
6. The greatest value of M is that it strengthens confidence in the reliability of G.
7. The presence of the "synonyms" prevents the possibility of reconstructing all the original words of Ben Sira.[59]

---

[54] See the sympathetic review by P. Skehan: 1966, pp. 260ff.
[55] Leiden: Brill, 1973.
[56] Ibid., pp. 98ff.
[57] Ibid., pp. 100ff.
[58] See pp. 98ff where he quotes with approval A. Volten's (*Studien zum Weisheitsbuch dei An II* Kopenhagen, 1937, p. 13) explanations of corruptions due to oral transmission.
[59] Pp. 100–12.

Rüger's study published in 1970, *Text und Textform im Hebraischen Sirach*,[60] argues that two forms of the Hebrew text developed, each along different lines due to "language interference." By comparing "doublets" (parallels within one manuscript) and "parallel traditions" (parallels between manuscripts) he shows that when two languages interfere with each other, certain patterns of changes take place. These changes in the Hebrew of Ben Sira produced two forms of the text, an older (Heb. I), and a younger (Heb. II). Heb. I relates to Heb. II as the Masoretic Text of the Hebrew Bible relates to the Targums.

At this point one could say there are three theories as to the development of the Hebrew recensions of Ben Sira:

1. The Hebrew materials (M, B, B marg.) are essentially genuine and the few differences are due to "partial retroversion" from Syriac (DiLella);
2. The Hebrew materials (M, B, B marg.) and Greek are genuine and their differences are due to changes during oral transmission (Middendorp);
3. The Hebrew materials are genuine but are now extant in primary (Heb. I) and secondary (Heb. II) forms; Heb. II is an inner development of the Hebrew materials and not due to retroversion (Rüger).

Theories (2) and (3) are certainly not incompatible and may in fact be two ways of saying the same thing. Yadin is neutral on the question of how the changes occurred, but does argue that B text and B margin represent different recensions of the Hebrew of Ben Sira which diverged from each other before the date of the Geniza manuscripts.[61]

[60] *Beihefte zur ZAW*, no. 112, de Gruyter, 1970.
[61] Yadin: 1965, p. 11.

2
The Syriac Versions, Manuscripts, and Editions of the Old Testament and the Place of Ben Sira in Them

A. THE SYRIAC VERSIONS, MANUSCRIPTS, AND EDITIONS OF THE OLD TESTAMENT[1]

The Old Syriac Version

The Origin of the Version. There are two competing theories as to the origin of the version known as the Old Syriac. In one, it is suggested that the Bible was translated into Syriac in the first century on the basis of a West Aramaic targum. This was supposedly done shortly after ca. A.D. 40 when the royal house of Adiabene was converted to Judaism.[2]

In the other, it is supposed that the Old Syriac originated with the beginnings of Christianity in Mesopotamia and was likewise based on a Palestinian targum.[3] Of the three centers of early Christianity in Syria—Antioch, Edessa, and Arbela—only Edessa and Arbela were truly Syrian, i.e., Syriac was the language of the people. According to an early tradition, perhaps legendary, Christianity was brought to Edessa by one Thaddaeus,[4] or

---

[1] For additional information, see Metzger: 1962, pp. 754f; 1977, ch. I; Vööbus: 1976, pp. 848–854; *List:* 1961; Peshitta Institute Communications: *VT* 1962, pp. 127f, 237f, 351; 1963, p. 349; 1977, pp. 508–511. I have given in this section even those Biblical versions and editions which do not contain Ben Sira; this will give an idea of the quantity of Syriac Biblical materials and the percent which contain Ben Sira.

[2] Baumstark had suggested that the Vorlage of the Peshitta could be traced to a Palestinian Targum in Baumstark: 1935, pp. 89–118. Cf. Kahle: 1959, pp. 265–273, esp. 272f; Würthwein: 1973, p. 87; Neusner: 1964, pp. 60–66.

[3] Vööbus: 1976, p. 848; Eissfeldt: 1965, pp. 699f. For information on the history of Christianity in Syria, cf. Metzger: 1977, pp. 4–10; McCullough, *A Short History of Syriac Christianity to the Rise of Islam* (forthcoming from Scholars Press, Chico, CA); Segal: 1970; Burkitt: 1904.

[4] Eusebius Pamphili, *Ecclesiastical History* I.13-1-9 (New York: Fathers of the Church, Inc., 1953), pp. 76–82.

Addai,[5] one of the seventy disciples sent out in the apostolic age. This would place the church's beginning in Syria in the first century, which is doubtful.

The introduction of Christianity to Arbela is dated to the reign of Emperor Trajan (98–117) in an early Chronicle of the city.[6] Again, Addai/Thaddaeus is named as the agent. It is probable that the first converts were from the Jewish community.

Whatever the reliability of the Addai/Thaddaeus tradition, Christianity is known to have been in existence in Syria shortly after the middle of the second century. And, whether the Old Syriac Version was first done by Jews or Christians, it is probably safe to say that the version existed, at least in part, in the second half of the second century A.D.

Manuscripts and Editions of the Old Syriac Version. There are no manuscripts of the Old Testament or Old Testament Apocrypha for the Old Syriac Version; only the Gospels are represented.

Curetonian Syriac MS:
    London, British Museum, Add. 14,451
    Royal Library of Berlin, Orient Quad. 528
    F. C. Burkitt, *Evangelion da-Mepharreshe; the Curetonian Syriac Gospels, re-edited, together with the readings of the Sinaitic Palimpsest,* 2 vols. (Cambridge, 1904). Fifth century; order—Matthew, Mark, John, Luke.

Sinai Syriac MS:
    Sinai, St. Catherine's Monastery, Syr. 30
    Agnes Smith Lewis, *The Old Syriac Gospels, or Evangelion da-Mepharreshe; being the text of the Sinai or Syro-Antiochian Palimpsest, including the latest additions and emendations, with the variants of the Curetonian Text* (London, 1910).

In view of this shortage of manuscript evidence for the Old Syriac Version, very little can be said about the Old Testament in Syriac at this stage. Either most of the manuscripts were destroyed when versions of the Peshitta were circulated[7] or only select books in Syriac ever existed (by request of private persons) and there was no complete Old Syriac Version.[8] Only the theory that the Old Syriac

---

[5] G. Phillips, ed. *Doctrine of Addai* (London, 1876). New edition in preparation, George Howard (Scholars Press, Chico, CA).

[6] Ca. A.D. 550, Metzger: 1977, p. 7.

[7] Lake: 1928, p. 140.

[8] Metzger: 1977, p. 47.

was used as a base for the Peshitta, the Palestinian Syriac Old Testament, and an Arabic version points to the existence of a whole version.[9]

The Peshitta

The Origin of the Version. The Peshitta was a "simple" version of the Syriac Bible prepared in place of the more complicated Syro-Hexaplaric Old Testament and the Harclean New Testament. The Old Testament was done by many hands beginning in the second or third century A.D. and, though close to the Masoretic Text, this revision is much affected by Targumic and Septuagintal influences. The Peshitta New Testament, completed in the late fourth century, is a revision of the Old Syriac on the basis of Greek; it excludes 2 Peter, 2 and 3 John, Jude and Revelation.[10]

The Peshitta Version was adopted by both Jacobites (Monophysites) and Nestorians since it was completed before Syriac Christianity divided into two communities after the middle of the fifth century. "From that time onward, there were four main recensions of the Peshitta text in use in the Syrian Church: firstly the . . . Nestorian and the remaining three, namely the Jacobite, Melchite and Maronite, representing the Western tradition."[11]

Manuscripts and Editions of the Peshitta[12]

Manuscripts. At the end of this chapter is a compilation from the appendix and main text of the *List of Old Testament Peshitta Manuscripts* of the Leiden Peshitta Institute and from "Peshitta Institute Communications" in subsequent volumes of *Vetus Testamentum.* The list given there (pp. 30–33) is not a complete list of all Peshitta manuscripts, but only of those which contain Ben Sira.

Recently identified Manuscripts:
Diyarbakir Mār Jā'qōb 1/1 1496 A.D. (OT), 1497/8 (NT) From Church of Mār Jā'qō b of Serūg in Diyarbakir Peshitta except Syro-hexaplar of I(III) Esdras and Tobit cf. Vööbus, *Discoveries,* pp. 11–17
Mār Behnām 1/1 1651 A.D. From Monastery of Mār Behnām near Mosul. Peshitta Old Testament and New Testament except Syro-hexaplar of I(III) Esdras and Tobit. Vööbus, Ibid.

---

[9] Vööbus: 1976, p. 849.

[10] This reflects the canon of the church at Antioch in the fourth and fifth centuries. The Peshitta also excludes Luke 22:17–18 and John 7:53–8:11. The missing books were included for the first time in Guy Michel Le Jay's *Paris Polyglot,* Vol. V (1630, 1633). Metzger: 1977, pp. 48, 54.

[11] Roberts: 1951, p. 223. In 431 A.D. the *person* and in 451 A.D. the *views* of Nestorius were condemned. McCullough, p. 241 of the manuscript.

[12] Metzger: 1962, pp. 754f and 1977, pp. 48–56; A. Vööbus: 1976, p. 849; Smend: 1906, II, pp. cxxxvi–cxlvi; 1907², pp. 271–275; List: 1961; Peshitta Institute Communications: 1962, 1963, 1977; Würthwein: 1973, p. 88.

Mardin Orth. L 1702–1718 A.D. From Mār Ḥanāyā Peshitta Old Testament except Syro-hexaplar of I(III) Esdras and Tobit. Vööbus, Ibid.
Mosul Orth. 177. From Syrian Orthodox Church in Mosul. Contains Ben Sira, I, II III Maccabees and the Book of Josippon in the Peshitta and I(III) Esdras and Tobit in the Syro-hexaplar.

Editions. All the major editions of the Peshitta are presented here. Those in which Ben Sira appears are marked with an asterisk (*).

*1645   Paris Polyglot, vol. 8. Michel Le Jays, *et al. Biblia Hebraica Samaritana, Chaldaica. Graeca. Syriaca. Latina. Arabica* (Paris, 1645). Peshitta text prepared by Gabriel Sionita (A.D. 1577–1648). Depends on a poor manuscript of the seventeenth century, *Codex Paris Syriaque,* 6 (17a5) from the Bibliothèque Nationale in Paris.

*1657   London Polyglot (S^W). Brian Walton, *et al., Biblia Sacra Polyglotta,* 4 (London, 1657). Reprint of the Paris polyglot but in worse form. Vol. 6, pp. 46ff, presents variants from codices Pocockianus (p), Usserianus (u), and Sebastian Hardy (h).

Editions for churches in Kurdistan, Lake Urmia and Northern Persia:

*1823   Lee (S^l) Samuel Lee, *Vetus Testamentum Syriace* (London, 1823). A reprint of the Paris and Walton Polyglots. West Syriac.

1852   Urmia (S^u) *ktb' qdyš' ddytq' 'tyqt'* By the American Protestant Missionary Society, 1852.

1954   Reprint, Trinitarian Bible Society, 1954.

*1887–91   Mosul (S^m) *Biblia sacra juxta versionem simplicem quae dicitur Pschitta,* tome 2 (Beirut, 1951), Sirach, pp. 204–255. By the Dominicans of Mosul, 1887–91; Beirut reprint, 1951. Based on manuscript of the seventeenth century A.D.; nearly complete agreement with London Polyglot.

*1814   Ben Ze'eb. Judah Löb Ben Ze'eb in 1814 published a Syriac text of Ben Sira from a "big Bible with translations into four languages." He says one version of Ben Sira was *blšwn 'rmyt* which he translated into Hebrew (*trgm 'rmvt*) while correcting misprints. The "big Bible" was probably Walton's Polyglot![13]

---

[13] McHardy: 1945–48, pp. 193f. McHardy says (p. 194), "Ben Ze'eb's edition, therefore, is but an imperfect copy of Walton's work, and it may be regarded as of no textual value."

*1861   Lagarde. P. A. de Lagarde, *Libri veteris testamenti apocryphi syriace* (Leipzig & London, 1861), pp. 2-51. Text of London Polyglot emended in many places to Codex Nitriensis.[14] Brit. Mus., Add. 12142, sixth century (7h3).

*1876ff   Ambrosianus (S^a). A. M. Ceriani, *Translatio Syra Pescitto Veteris Testamenti ex Codice Ambrosiano Sec. fere VI. photolithographice edita*, 2, 4 (Milan, 1878). Based on Codex Milan, Ambr., B.21. Inf. (7a1) of the sixth-seventh century. Very close to MT.

1904, 1914 Barnes. W. E. Barnes, *The Peshitta Psalter according to the West Syrian Text edited with an Apparatus Criticus* (Cambridge, 1904; London, 1914). Based on the Ambrosian codex published by Ceriani in 1878.

1914   Barnes. *Pentateuchus syriace post Samuelem Lee, recognovit, emendavit, edidit W. E. Barnes, adiuvantibus C. W. Mitchell, I. Pinkerton* (London, 1914). Fifth-sixth century manuscripts.

*1968   Vattioni. Francesco Vattioni, *Ecclesiastico. Testo ebraico con apparato critico e versioni greca, latina e siriaca* (Instituto Orientale di Napoli, 1968). Reproduces virtually completely Brit. Mus., Add. 12142 (7h3), which was used by Lagarde.[15]

*1966ff   Peshitta Institute. *The Old Testament in Syriac According to The Peshitta Version* (The Peshitta Institute of the University of Leiden).

         1966:   Sample edition: Song of Songs (J. A. Emerton), Toblt (J. C. H. Lebram), 4 Ezra (R. J. Bidawid)

         1972:   General Preface to the complete work (P. A. H. deBoer; W. Baars)

         1972:   Part IV, fascicle 6 (some apocrypha and pseudepigrapha) (H. Schneider, W. Baars, J. C. H. Lebram)

         *   Critical text of Ben Sira in preparation by M. M. Winter (based on Codex Ambrosianus).[16]

The *editio princeps* of the Syriac of Ben Sira is thus the text of Gabriel Sionita. This text was used as the basis of the Paris (1645) and London (1657)

---

[14] See R. Smend: 1906, II, pp. cxli-cxlii.

[15] M. M. Winter (personal communication, Dec. 17, 1977) says that "the London MS which de Lagarde used is better than Ambrosianus. Its sign is 7h3, and you can use it with confidence."

[16] See n. 15.

polyglots, and therefore also as the basis for the editions of Lee (1823), Urmia (1852), Mosul (1887–91) and Lagarde (1861). The new Peshitta Institute edition will be based on Codex Ambrosianus.

The Philoxenian Version

The Origin of the Version. Polycarp, chorepiscopus of Bishop Philoxenus of Mabbug in Syria, produced a version of the Syriac Bible by revising the Peshitta Old Testament according to a Lucianic recension of the LXX.[17] The New Testament was also revised to accord with Greek manuscripts, and the books of 2 Peter, 2 and 3 John, Jude, and Revelation were included. This translation was done in 507–508 A.D. for the purpose of revising the Peshitta Version along lines more acceptable to the Jacobite (Monophysite) Christians.

Manuscripts and Editions of the Philoxenian Version. The only surviving manuscripts of the version which are known to the truly Philoxenian are New Testament manuscripts which contain 2 Peter, 2 and 3 John, Jude, and Revelation.[18]

1630	Edward Pococke. *Epistolae quatuor, Petris secunda, Iohannis secunda et tertia ed Judae fratris Jacobi una,* Lugduni Batavorum, 1630. Oxford, Bodleian Library, Or. 119 (ca. 1610 A.D.).
1909	John Gwynn. *Remnants of the Later Syriac Versions of the Bible; Part I: New Testament. The Four Minor Catholic Epistles in the Original Philoxenian Version of the Sixth Century, and the History of the Woman Taken in Adultery* (London and Oxford, 1909; reprinted in Amsterdam, 1974).
1627	Ludovicus de Dieu. Leiden University, cod. Scaliger 18 Syr. The Book of Revelation from this manuscript has been used in printed editions of the Syriac New Testament from the time of the Paris Polyglot.
1897	John Gwynn. *The Apocalypse of St. John, in a Syriac Version Hitherto Unknown* (Dublin, 1897). Manchester, John Rylands Library, Earl of Crawford Syriac New Testament Manuscript (twelfth or thirteenth century A.D.).

As for the text of the Old Testament in the Philoxenian Version, only indirect and fragmentary evidence is known. Vööbus reports a quotation from

---

[17] Eissfeldt: 1965, p. 701; Metzger: 1977, pp. 63–66; see Fox: 1979, for a study of the Matthew-Luke commentary of Philoxenus and its bearing on the question of the Philoxenian Version, esp. pp. 19–24.

[18] Metzger: 1977, p. 66.

this version in a scholion of Syro-Hexaplar MS Mil. C313f, a fragment of Isaiah in Brit. Mus. Add. 17,106, and quotations from Isaiah in Moshe of Aggel's Syriac translation of Cyril's *Glaphyra*.[19] He believes the Philoxenian Version of Isaiah was based on a form of the text older than the Peshitta and was revised according to the Lucianic LXX.[20]

The Syro-Hexapla

The Origin of the Version. Paul, bishop of Tella de-Mauzelath, fled Mesopotamia upon threat from the Persians to a Syrian monastery near Alexandria in Egypt.[21] Here he produced a Syriac version from the Greek text of the fifth column of Origen's Hexapla in 616–617. The version is known as the "Syro-Hexapla" and is a very cautious rendering of Origen's text, preserving even the Aristarchian signs and variants from Aquila, Symmachus, Theodotion, and (in the Psalms) from Quinta and Sexta. This version was used by both Jacobite and Nestorian scholars.[22]

Manuscripts and Editions of the Syro-Hexapla. The editions of Ceriani and Rahlfs form "the basis of most of what we know about Paul of Tella's translation of the Old Testament."[23]

Andreas Masius (1514–1573) had a manuscript of the Syro-Hexapla which contained part of the Pentateuch and historical books, though it is now lost.[24] Most likely, it is the first part of which Milan, Ambr. C313 inf. (published by Ceriani, 1874) forms the second part. All that is known of Masius' manuscript can be found in Rahlfs and de Lagarde (cited below).[25]

1874 A. M. Ceriani. *Codex syro-hexaplaris Ambrosianus photolithographice editus* (Milan, 1874). Milan, MS Ambr. C313 inf., eighth or ninth century. Contains the prophets and writings, though the psalms in this version are not hexaplaric. Sirach is included (f86a–96b), though Ziegler claims chapter 51 never stood in the manuscript.[26]

[19] Vööbus: 1976, p. 849.

[20] Ibid.

[21] Baumstark: Bonn, 1922; Reprint, Berlin, 1968, pp. 186–188. Cf. also John Gwynn: 1887, pp. 266–271; Vööbus: 1971, pp. 33–36.

[22] Baars: 1968, p. 2; Vööbus: 1971, for a survey of the preservation of the Hexapla and Syro-Hexapla and new discoveries.

[23] Baars: 1968, p. 9; see Vööbus: 1971, pp. 68ff for recent additions.

[24] Partially preserved in quotations in his Syriac lexicon *Syronum Peculium* (Antwerp Polyglot, 1569).

[25] Baars: 1968, p. 4 for proposed contents of the Masius manuscript.

[26] Ziegler: 1965, p. 58. However, Baars (1968, p. 5 n. 3) points out that Ceriani noted on p. 60 of his edition of Ambrosianus that a leaf was missing after folio 96. This probably contained Ben Sira 51.

1892   A. Rahlfs' re-issue of de Lagarde's publication of the Paris and
            London manuscripts of the Syro-Hexapla (*Veteris Testamenti
            ab Origine recensiti fragmenta*, Göttingen, 1880), *Bibliothecae
            Syriacae* (Göttingen, 1892), pp. 121ff.

A number of Syro-hexaplaric manuscripts have been identified in recent
years. I will mention here only those which contain the book of Ben Sira.
Publications by Vööbus, Goshen-Gottstein and Baars provide comprehensive
information on the new discoveries.[27] It is also known that the Syro-Hexapla was
quoted in the lectionaries and exegetical works.[28]

London, B. M., Add. 7145, fol. I "Single damaged leaf that is difficult to
    read."[29] Mixed up with Peshitta texts. Syrohexaplaric text of Gen
    26:26-31; Jos 22:1-6; Prov 2:1-12., *Sir.* 31:8.

Mardin, Syr. Ortho. Bishopric, 47 1569 A.D., f69a, 1.26-69b, 1.10 Includes
    Sir. 51:6-11. Written in monastery of Mar Azazael near Mardin in a
    Serta hand.

Mardin, Syr. Ortho. Bishopric, 48 1738/1739 A.D.[30]

Mosul, Orth. 177 Contains Ben Sira, I, II and III Maccabees, the book of
    Josippon, I (III) Esdras and Tobit. Ben Sira is introduced: "Again, the
    Book of Wisdom of Īšō'bar Šem'on who is called Bar 'Asīrā." I (III)
    Esdras is introduced: "according to the tradition of the edition of the
    Seventy" and Tobit: "likewise according to the tradition and the Sep-
    tuagint version."[31] This should probably be taken to mean that Ben
    Sira is *not* Syro-hexaplaric in this manuscript. Vööbus mentions three
    other newly identified Syriac manuscripts containing "extracanonical"
    books; in these only I (III) Esdras and Tobit are identified as
    Syro-hexaplaric.[32]

The Version of Jacob of Edessa

The Origin of the Version. The last Syriac version of the Old Testament to
be mentioned is that of Jacob of Edessa (d. ca. 708).[33] This work was done

---

[27] Vööbus: 1970; 1971; 1976, p. 850; Baars: 1968; Goshen-Gottstein: 1964, pp. 230f.
[28] The Mardin MSS Orth. 47, 48 are lectionaries.
[29] Baars: 1968, p. 17.
[30] Ibid., pp. 18f, 30; Vööbus: 1970, pp. 20-26; 1976, p. 850.
[31] Vööbus: 1970, p. 17.
[32] Ibid., pp. 12-16.
[33] This is not the place to mention the extensive influence of Ben Sira in Jewish and
Christian literature or its citation by authors of such works. Cf. Vattioni: 1968, pp. xxx-xl.

toward the end of Jacob's life, in the monastery of Tell'ada. A revision based on the Peshitta and the Syro-hexapla, parts of the Pentateuch, Samuel, Kings, Daniel and Ezekiel are preserved in known manuscripts.[34]

Manuscripts and Editions of the Version of Jacob of Edessa.[35] There is no known manuscript evidence for the existence of Ben Sira in this version.

The Palestinian Syriac Version[36]

The Origin of the Version. The Syro-Palestinian Melchite Christians made a translation of the Greek Old and New Testaments into a Palestinian Aramaic dialect somewhat different from Syriac. It is really in a western Aramaic dialect closer to Jewish Palestinian Aramaic than Edessean Syriac, but the script is an archaic Estrangela Syriac.[37] For this reason, the Palestinian Syriac Version is placed here, after the proper Syriac versions.

The dates for the origin of this version range from 300 A.D. to 700 A.D. It is suggested that the version existed in an oral form from translations of the Greek Bible used in Melchite worship,[38] perhaps as early as the fourth century, and was put in written form in the fifth century,[39] or shortly thereafter.[40] An Arab author, Ibn Ishaq, quoted from the version in ca. 700 A.D.[41]

Manuscripts and Editions of the Palestinian Syriac Version.[42] The Palestinian Syriac Version is known mainly from codices (A, B and C) of three lectionaries, some forty-two psalms and fragments of psalms,[43] and fragments of other Biblical books.

A   Gospel Lectionary (Vatican, 1030 A.D.)
     S. E. Assemani and J. S. Assemani, *Bibliothecae Apostolicae Vaticanae codicum Manuscriptorum catalogus,* Pars I, Tom. ii (Rome, 1758), pp. 70–103.

---

[34] Vööbus: 1976, p. 850.

[35] Ibid.

[36] Formerly known as the Jerusalem Syriac Version.

[37] Metzger: 1977, p. 76; Vööbus: 1976, p. 849.

[38] Metzger: 1977, p. 77, based on citation from St. Egeria (Aetheria); S. Silvia, *Peregrinatio,* xlvii.3 (*Corpus Scriptorum Ecclesiasticorum Latinorum,* Vienna. xxxix.99, 13–21).

[39] M.-J. Lagrange: 1925, pp. 481–504.

[40] Vööbus: 1954, pp. 126f. Vööbus also mentions a reference in Jerome to the burial of St. Paula (d. 404) in Bethlehem, "Graeco Latino Syroque sermone psalms in ordine personabant" (*Epistulae* cviii.29), which may be a hint of the existence of this version, Vööbus: 1976, p. 850.

[41] Vööbus: 1976, p. 850.

[42] Metzger: 1977, pp. 78–80; Vööbus: 1954, p. 323.

[43] Vööbus: 1976, p. 849. I personally have not been able to find manuscript evidence of these Syriac psalms.

J. G. C. Adler, *Novi Testamenti versiones Syriacae simplex, Philoxeniana et Hierosolymitana* (Copenhagen, 1789), pp. 135–201.

Francesco Miniscalchi Erizzo, *Evangeliarium Hierosolymitanum*, I–II (Verona, 1861–1864).

Paul de Lagarde, *Evangeliarium Hierosolymitanum, Bibliothecae syriacae quae ad philologiam sacram pertinent* (Göttingen, 1892), pp. 258–402.

B,C   Monastery of St. Catherine, Mt. Sinai (1104, 1118 A.D.)

A. S. Lewis, *A Palestinian Syriac Lectionary, Containing Lessons from the Pentateuch, Job, Proverbs, Acts and Epistles* (London, 1897).

A. S. Lewis and M. D. Gibson, *The Palestinian Syriac Lectionary of the Gospels, Re-edited from Two Sinai Mss. and from P. de Lagarde's Edition of the 'Evangeliarium Hierosolymitanum'* (London, 1899).

In addition to the lectionaries, fragments of some Biblical books have been preserved in manuscripts of the Palestinian Syriac Version. Some of these have only recently been published.

A. S. Lewis, *Codex Climaci Rescriptus, Fragments of Sixth Century Palestinian Syriac Texts of the Gospels, of the Acts of the Apostles and of St. Paul's Epistles* (Cambridge, 1909). 2 Thessalonians and Philemon are missing, but James and 2 Peter are present.

Khirbet Mird (Luke 3:1, 3–4; Acts 10:28f, 32–41; Col 1:16–18, 20ff)[44]

R. deVaux, "Fouille au Khirbet Qumran," *RB* 60 (1953) pp. 83–106, Pls. II–VII.

G. R. H. Wright, "The Archaeological Remains at El Mird in the Wilderness of Judaea, with an Appendix, 'The Monastery of Kastellion,' by J. T. Milik." *Biblica* 42 (1961), pp. 1–27, Pls. I–XII, Figs. 1–6.

Charles Perrot, "Un fragment christo-palestinien découvert à Khirbet Mird," *RB* 70 (1963), pp. 506–555.

Friedrich Schulthess, *Christlich-Palästinische Fragmente aus der Omajjaden-Moschee zu Damascus.* Abh. d. Kgl. Gen. d. Wiss. zu Göttingen. Philol. hist. Kl. N.F. VIII 3 (Berlin, 1905), pp. 39ff. 45:25–46:8 (Sir.)

H. Duensing, *Christlich-palästinisch-aramäische Texte und Fragmente* (Göttingen, 1906, reprinted, Jerusalem, 1971), p. 126 12:18; 13:3, 4a, 7 (Sir.)

---

[44] Eissfeldt: 1965, p. 640; Metzger: 1977, pp. 79f.

B. THE PLACE OF BEN SIRA IN THE SYRIAC OLD TESTAMENT

As the information above indicates, a Syriac Version of Ben Sira appears in all the major editions of the whole Syriac Peshitta Bible, except the Urmia edition (1852, 1954), and will appear in a complete critical edition in the new Peshitta Institute *The Old Testament in Syriac According to the Peshitta Version* (1966ff). The Urmia edition excluded Ben Sira along with all other apocryphal books.

There is no way to know whether Ben Sira existed in Syriac before the Peshitta Version. The only textual evidence for the Old Syriac Version is two manuscripts of the Gospels. None of the Old Testament, Apocrypha, or New Testament epistles has yet appeared. Only the possibility, mentioned above, that the Old Syriac was used as a base for the Peshitta, the Palestinian Syriac Old Testament, and an Arabic version, and that the Philoxenian Old Testament goes back to a version older than the Peshitta, gives a clue to a Syriac Old Testament before the Peshitta.[45] And even this does not guarantee that Ben Sira was a part of it.

Only parts of the Pentateuch, Job, Proverbs and some Psalms and other books are extant in the Old Testament portions of the Palestinian Syriac Version. The fact, though, that lectionaries existed in this version may indicate that at one time a whole Christian Palestinian Syriac Version was known and used. Ben Sira is known from several passages in this version.[46]

Ben Sira is present in the best known MS of the Syro-hexapla, Ambr. C313 inf. of the eighth or ninth century A.D., and in part in several recently discovered manuscripts. This is more a witness to its place in the Greek Bible, of course, than in the Syriac Bible.

There is no textual evidence that Ben Sira existed in Jacob of Edessa's version, but since that version was a revision from the Peshitta and Syro-hexapla, Ben Sira was probably there if the version was complete.

The faults of the Syriac Peshitta antedate the oldest existing manuscripts (Ambrosianus and Brit. Mus. Add. 12142) and are repeated in the later manuscripts that form the bases for the polyglots and the Mosul Bible.[47] Thus, with only slight exception, the manuscript tradition of the Syriac of Ben Sira is uniform.

Smend, following the dictum of Rahlfs to establish the Syriac text of the Peshitta from agreements between Jacobite and Nestorian manuscripts, compared a number of Syriac manuscripts of Ben Sira in order to establish an original and reliable text.[48] The following is a summary of his investigation and conclusions:

---

[45] See above, Chapter 2, nn. 9 and 20.
[46] Schulthess: 1905, pp. 39–40; Duensing: 1906, p. 126.
[47] DiLella: 1966, p. 17.
[48] Smend 1906, II, pp. cxliii–cxlvi; 1907², pp. 271–275.

Mas. I (Nestorian, 899 A.D.): BM Add. 12138 (9ml). 100 passages depart from Lagarde; 4/5 of these coincide with the Polyglot. S^a and S^{berol} more often agree with Mas. I and S^w.

Other Nestorian Mss: BM Add. 7150, 1820 A.D. (19cl); BM Add. 14, 440, X–XI (IIcl); Vatican Sir. 3, 1558 A.D. (16cl); Vatican Sir. 6, XII (12h2).

Walton's London Polyglot, S^w (Jacobite, 1657 A.D.). Based on Paris Polyglot.

Codex Ambrosianus, S^a.

Lagarde: Based on S^w and Nitriensis (BM Add. 12142).

Mas. 11 (Jacobite, IX–X): BM Add. 12178. 80 passages deviate from Lagarde; ½ are unique, none of them agrees with Nitriensis.

Other Jacobite MSS: Berlin Sachau 30, 1821 AD (19gl) = S^{berol}.

Mosul Bible, S^m: Hardly Nestorian; agrees too often with Polyglot.

Upon comparison of the above materials, Smend concludes:

(1)   That Lagarde too hastily rejected Polyglot readings;

(2)   Where Mas. I (Nestorian) and S^w (Jacobite) agree is the true original Syriac text of Ben Sira;

(3) S^a and S^{berol} (Jacobite) often agree with Mas I (Nestorian) and S^w (Jacobite) and almost always with S^m (not Nestorian).

For the material used by this writer, one can say that the Mosul Bible (S^m) and Ambrosianus (S^a) agree closely. S^m and the text of Lagarde (which also appears in Vattioni's polyglot) hardly deviate at all. The individual cases will be discussed in Chapter IV below, "Comparative Translation: Ben Sira 39:27–44:17."

A list of Peshitta manuscripts
that contain Ben Sira follows
on pages 30–33.

Sigla	MS and Location
7a1	Milan, Ambr., B. 21. Inf.
7h3	London, B.M., Add. 12, 142
7pk2	Cambridge, Un. L., T.-S. 12.743
8a1	Paris, N.L., Syr. 341
9c1	Paris, N.L., Syr. 372
9m1	London, B.M., Add. 12, 138
10c1	New Haven, A.O.S.L., B47b
10c2	Rome, Vat. L., Borg. sir. 93
10m1	London, B.M., Add. 12, 178
10m2	London, B.M., Add. 14, 667
10m3	Rome, Vat. L., Vat. sir. 152
11c1	London, B.M., Add. 14, 440
11m1	Chicago, Or. Inst. L.
11m2	London, B.M., Add. 7183
11m4	Mossul, Church of St. Thomas
11m5	Paris, N.L., Syr. 64
11m6	Rome, Vat. L., Barb. or. 118
11m7	Rome, Vat. L., Borg. sir. 117
12a1	Cambridge, Un. L., Oo. 1. 1, 2
12h2	Rome, Vat. L., Vat. sir. 6
12k2	London, B.M., Add. 14, 730
12m1	London, B.M., Add. 14, 482
13a1	Paris, N.L., Syr. 9
13c1	Cambridge (USA) Harv. Sem. Mus., Syr. Ms. 118
13m1	Lund, Un. L., Mass. ms.
14c1	Cambridge, Un. L., Add. 1964
14c2	Kirkuk, Archepiscopal Library
17/15a1	Paris, N.L., Syr. 11
15c1	Woodbrooke, S.O.C.L., Ming. Syr. 504
16c1	Rome, Vat. L., Vat. sir. 3
16g3	Rome, Vat. L., Borg. Sir. 55
16g5	Rome, Vat. L., Vat. sir. 433
18/16g6	Woodbrooke, S.O.C.L., Ming. syr. 279
16h2	Rome, Vat. L., Barb. or. 76
17a1	London, B.M., Egerton 704
17a2	Milan, Ambr., A. 145. Inf.
17a3	Oxford, Bodl. L., Bod. Or. 141

Date	Folia/Pages
VI-VII	Sir, f223ᵃ–237ᵇ
VI-VII	Sir (missing 42:11–26; 46:4–18), f1ᵃ–73ᵇ
VI-VIII(?) rescr. XII-XIII	Sir (13:2–14:1), f1ᵃ–2ᵇ
VII-VIII	Sir, f218ᵃ–227ᵇ
VIII-X Nestorian	Sir (missing 10:16–14:15) f110ᵃ–132ᵇ
A.D. 899 Nestorian	Sir, f150ᵃ–160ᵇ
IX-XI Nestorian	Sir, f189ᵃ–220ᵃ
IX-XI Nestorian	Sir (missing 10:5–11:28; 31:8–35:16; 49:4–51:30), f68ᵃ–87ᵇ
IX-X	Sir, f144ᵃ–152ᵃ
X	Sir (missing 4:17–20.14), f2ʰ–4ʰ
A.D. 979/80	Sir, f113ᵃ–118ᵇ
X-XI Nestorian	Sir, f250ᵇ–289ᵇ
A.D. 1004	Sir, p213–223
XI	Sir, f79ᵇ–82ᵇ
A.D. 1014	Sir, f108ᵃ–112ᵇ
XI	Sir (missing 15:20–23:15), f97ᵃ–98ᵇ, 104ᵃ–107ᵃ
X-XI	Sir, f91ᵃ–97ᵇ
A.D. 1868 < 1014 copied from 11m4	Sir, f213ᵇ–223ᵃ
XII	Sir, f200ᵃ–208ᵃ
XII Nestorian	Sir, f1ᵃ–40ᵇ
XII	Sir (2:1–5, 6ᵇ–11), f87ᵇ–88ᵃ VT XII (1962) p. 351
XI-XII	Sir, f61ᵃ–64ᵇ
XIII	Sir, f247ᵇ–258ᵇ
XII-XIV Nestorian	Sir, f136ᵇ–165ᵃ
A.D. 1204/5	Sir, f194ᵇ–204ᵃ
XIII-XV Nestorian	Sir, f159ᵃ–184ᵇ
XIII-XIV Nestorian	Sir (missing 1:1–37; 12:3–13:24) f229ᵃ–257ᵇ, 2,4,3,5,6,258ᵃ
XV	Sir, f234ᵇ–265ᵃ
XIV-XV	Sir (missing 13:16–17:21; 22:2–23:3; 46:20–51:30), f69ᵃ–98ᵇ, 100
A.D. 1558 Nestorian	Sir, f171ᵃ–200ᵃ
A.D. 1558	Sir, f126ᵇ–143ᵇ
XVI	Sir, pp. 289–346
XV-XVI	Sir, f320ᵃ–335ᵇ
XVI (A.D. 1586?)	Sir, f8ᵃ–49ᵇ
XVII	Sir, f306ᵃ–320ᵃ
Part II (A.D. 1615)	Sir, f44ᵃ–76ᵃ
A.D. 1627	Sir, f516ᵃ–544ᵃ

Sigla	MS and Location
17a4	Oxford, Bodl. L.. Poc. 391
17a5	Paris, N.L., Syr. 6
17a6	Paris, N.L., Syr. 8
17a7	Rome, Bibl. Casan., Ms. 194
17a8	Rome, Vat. L., Vat. sir. 7
17a9	Rome, Vat, L., Vat. sir. 8
17a10	Rome, Vat. L., Vat. sir. 258
17a11	Rome, Vat. L., Vat. sir. 461
17c1	Mossul, Chald. Patrl, 112
17c2	Woodbrooke, S.O.C.L., Ming. syr. 552
17g2	Milan, Ambr. Y. 8. Sup.
17g3	Paris, N.L., Syr. 243
17g5	Rome, Vat. L., Vat. sir. 436
17h1	Florence, Med. Laur., Or. 254
18c1	Cambridge, Un. L., Add. 1963
18c2	Cambridge, Un. L., Oo. 1.10
18g3	Cambridge, Un. L., Oo. 1.39
18hj1	Oxford, Bodl. L., Lamb. 4
19c1	London, B.M., Add. 7150
19c2	London, B.M., Or. 4396
19c3	London, B.M., Or. 9350
19c4	Woodbrooke, S.O.C.L., Ming. syr. 437
19g1	Berlin, G.S.L., Sachau 70
19g5	Rome, Vat. L., Borg. sir. 116
19g7	Woodbrooke, S.O.C.L., Ming. syr. 63
19g8	Cambridge, Christ's College, Dd. 7.13

Date	Folia/Pages
A.D. 1614	Sir, f322^b–341^b
XVII	Sir, f474^a–498^a
XVII	Sir, f197^a–211^a
XVII	Sir, f264^b–280^a
XVI-XVII	Sir, f319^a–335^b
XVI-XVII	Sir, f238^a–250^b
XVI-XVII	Sir, f466^b–486^a
A.D. 1666/7	Sir, f280^a–295^b
A.D. 1696 Nestorian	Sir, (missing??), f186^b–219^b
XVII Nestorian	Sir, f208^b–241^b
XVI-XVII Maronite	Sir, f33^a–120^a
A.D. 1610	Sir (mostly illegible), f?49^a–293^a
A.D. 1623 Maronite	Sir, pp. 442–509
XVI-XVII (before A.D. 1614)	Sir, f1^a–60^b
XVIII Nestorian	Sir, f214^b–249^a
XVII-XVIII Nestorian	Sir, f193^a–237^b
XVII-XVIII Nestorian	Sir (portions are repeated), f123^a–213^b
XVII-XVIII	Sir, (31:16–23), f36^b; Sir (41:1–4), f37^b–38^b
A.D. 1820 Nestorian	Sir, f210^a–243^b
A.D. 1808 Nestorian	Sir, f212^b–245^b
A.D. 1853 Nestorian	Sir, f215^a–252^b
A.D. 1855 Nestorian	Sir, f216^b–253^a
A.D. 1821	Sir, f1^a–58^a
A.D. 1868	Sir, f221^b–249^a
A.D. 1821	Sir, f352^b–37?^{b}
A.D. 1818	Sir (missing 41:4–14), f289^b–323^b

3

A Comparison of the Greek, Hebrew and Syriac Texts for Absence or Presence of Verses

A. INTRODUCTION

The lengthy chart presented in this chapter is based on a careful comparison of the Syriac, Hebrew and Greek materials available to this author for Ben Sira 39:27–44:17. All of these materials have been translated[1] and the chart thus represents correspondences determined by comparison of the actual wording of the texts.

There are two columns for Syriac, in order to show the relationship between the two most easily available Syriac texts — that of the Mosul Bible and that found in Vattioni's polyglot.[2] The Hebrew appears in three columns — B for MSB of the Cairo Geniza, M for the Masada text of *The Historical Dictionary of the Hebrew Language*, Y for Yadin's edition of the Masada text. The Greek, G^I, stands in the last column. Yadin's edition of the Masada text, Y, is presented next to M for two reasons: first, because there are some slight differences between the two editions and second, because additional information about the state of the manuscript is indicated by Yadin. This information is conveyed by certain notes and sigla in the chart.[3]

The numbers for verses in the chart come from the editions of the texts which were consulted. This will facilitate matching of verses from one edition or version to the next. In the right-hand column, G^I, are the standard verse numbers used by almost everyone in citing Ben Sira. They come from J. Ziegler, *Sapientia Iesu Filii Sirach,* a system ultimately derived from H. B. Swete, *The Old Testament in Greek According to the Septuagint* (Cambridge, University Press, 1901^3).[4]

---

[1] See Chapter 4.
[2] See "Texts Used" for more details.
[3] See "Sigla."
[4] The system is also used in M. M. Winter, *A Concordance to the Peshitta Version of Ben Sira* (Leiden: Brill, 1976) and in *The Old Testament in Syriac According to the Peshitta Version* (the Peshitta Institute of the University of Leiden).

B. TEXTS USED

S^L   Syriac text of de Lagarde as presented in Francesco Vattioni, *Ecclesiastico. Testo ebraico con apparato critico e versioni greca, latina e siriaca.* Pubblicazioni del Seminario di Semitistica, Test I. Instituto Orientale di Napoli, 1968. Reproduces virtually completely the London MS 14142 (7h3) used by P. de Lagarde in *Libri Veteris Testamenti apocryphi syriace* (Lipsiae-Londini, 1861).

S^m   Syriac text of the Mosul Bible as presented in the Beirut reprint, *Biblia Sacra. Juxta Versionem Simplicem quae dicitur Pschitta.* Tomus Secundus. Beryti: Typis Typographiae Catholicae, 1951.

B   Manuscript B and marginal readings as presented in *The Book of Ben Sira. Text, Concordance and an Analysis of the Vocabulary. The Historical Dictionary of the Hebrew Language.* Jerusalem: The Academy of the Hebrew Language and the Shrine of the Book, 1973.

Bm   Margin of manuscript B.

M   The Masada manuscript as presented in *The Book of Ben Sira. Text, Concordance and an Analysis of the Vocabulary. The Historical Dictionary of the Hebrew Language.* Jerusalem: The Academy of the Hebrew Language and the Shrine of the Book, 1973.

Y   The Masada manuscript as presented in Yigael Yadin, *The Ben Sira Scroll from Masada. With Introduction, Emendations and Commentary.* Jerusalem: The Israel Exploration Society and the Shrine of the Book, 1965.

G^I   The Greek text as presented in Joseph Ziegler, ed. *Sapientia Iesu Filii Sirach. Vetus Testamentum Graecum. Auctoritate Societatis Litterarum Gottingensis editum.* Vol. XII, 2. Göttingen, Vandenhoeck and Ruprecht, 1965.

C. SIGLA

[ ]	Reading restored by editor from some traces
X	Verse exists in one or more of the texts consulted, but not in the one marked with an X
...	Trace of a reading, but unintelligible
...39.27	Trace of a reading; enough present to give some meaning
=	Present in close form
~	Present, but not in exact form
?	Difficulty in the translation
LOST	Destroyed from manuscript M. Originally present, but now LOST
N.P.	NOT PRESENT, i.e. never a part of manuscript M

S^L	S^m	B	M	Y	G^I(Ziegler's)
39:27 =	39:32 =	39:27 =	39:27 =	[39:27] =	39:27
39:28 =	39:33 =	39:28a =	39:28a =	[39:28] =	39:28ab
39:28 =	39:34 =	X =	39:28b =	[39:28c] =	39:28cd
39:29 =	39:35 =	39:29 =	39:29 =	[39:29] =	39:29
39:30 =	39:36 =	39:30 =	... =	[39:30c] =	39:30
X =	X =	39:30c =	... =	[30:30] =	39:31b
39:31 =	39:37 =	39:31 =	... =	[39:31] ~	39:31ac
39:32 =	39:38 =	39:32 =	... =	[39.32] =	39:32
39:33 =	39:39 =	39:33	X	LOST =	39:33
39:34 =	39:40 =	39:34	X	LOST =	39:34
39:35 =	39:41 =	39:35	X	LOST =	39:35
40:1 =	40:1a ~	40:1a	X	LOST =	40:1a
40:1 =	40:1b =	40:1b	X	LOST =	40:1b
40:2 =	40:2	X	X	LOST =	40:2
40:3 =	40:3 =	40:3	X	LOST =	40:3
40:4 =	40:3a =	40:4	X	LOST =	40:4
40:5 =	40:3b =	40:5a	X	LOST =	40:5a
40:5 =	40:5,6a =	40:5b	X	LOST	40:5b
X	X	40:6a	X	LOST =	40:6a
40:6 =	40:6b ~	40:6b	X	LOST =	40:6b
	(B)40:6a =	(G^I)40:6a			
	(B)40:6b =	(G^I)40:6b			
	(S^L,S^m)40:6 /6b	blends the doublet			
40:7 =	40:7 =	40:7	X	LOST =	40:7
40:8 =	40:8 =	40:8	...	LOST =	40:8
X	X	40:9	X	LOST =	40:9
X	X	40:10	X	[40:10] =	40:10
40:11 =	40:11 =	40:11 =	40:11 =	[40:11] =	40:11
40:12 =	40:12 =	X =	40:12 =	[40:12] =	40:12
40:13 =	40:13 =	40:13	40:13 =	[40:13] =	40:13
40:14 =	40:14ab =	40:14 =	40:14 =	40:14 ?	40:14
	(Syriac expansion?)				
40:15 =	40:15a =	40:15 =	40:15 =	40:15 =	40:15
40:16 =	40:15b =	40:16 =	40:16 =	40:16 =	40:16
40:17 =	40:17a ~	40:17 =	40:17 =	40:17 =	40:17
40:17 =	40:17b =	40:18ab =	40:18ab =	40:18 =	40:18ab
	(1/2 missing in Syriac)				
40:18 =	40:18(AB)=	40:19a(AB)=	40:19a(AB)=	40:19 =	40:19(A→C)
40:19 =	40:19(DC)=	40:19b(DC)	...	[40:19c]	X
40:20 =	40:20 =	40:20	X	LOST =	40:20
40:21 =	40:21 =	40:21	X	LOST =	40:21
40:22 =	40:22 =	40:22	X	LOST =	40:22

S^L	S^m	B	M	Y	G^I(Ziegler's)
40:23 =	40:23 =	40:23	X	LOST =	40:23
40:24 =	40:24 =	40:24	X	LOST =	40:24
40:25 =	40:25 =	40:25	X	LOST =	40:25
40:26 =	40:26 =	40:26a	...	[40:26a] =	40:26a
40:26 =	40:27 =	40:26b	...1/2	[40:28b] =	40:26b
40:26 =	40:28a	X	X	N.P.	X
40:27 =	40:28b =	40:27	...1/2	[40:26] =	40:27
40:28 =	40:29	40:28 =	...1/2	[40:26c] =	40:28
40:29 =	40:30 =	40:29a =	... =	[40:29] =	40:29a
40:29 =	40:31 ~	40:29b	...1/2 =	[40:29c] =	40:29b
40:30 =	40:32 =	40:30 =	40:30 =	40:30 =	40:30
↑	↑	↑	↑	↑	↑
41:1 =	41:1 =	41:1a =	41:1a =	41:1 =	41:1a
41:1 =	41:2 =	41:1b =	41:1b =	41:1c =	41:1b
41:2 =	41:3 =	41:2a =	41:2a =	41:2 =	41:2a
41:2 =	41:4 ~	41:2b =	41:2b =	41:2c ~	41:2b
41:3 =	41:5 =	41:3 =	41:3 =	41:3 =	41:3
41:4 =	41:6 =	41:4a =	41:4a =	41:4 =	41:4a
X	X	41:4b =	41:4b =	41:4c =	41:4b
41:5 =	41:8 ~	41:5 =	41:5 =	41:5 ~	41:5
41:6 =	41:9 =	41:6 =	...41:6 =	[41:6] =	41:6
41:7 =	41:10 =	41:7 =	...41:7 =	41:7 =	41:7
41:8 =	41:11 =	... ~	41:8 =	41:8 =	41:8
X	X	41:9a =	...41:9a =	41:9 =	41:9ab
41:9 =	41:12	X	X	N.P.	X
41:9 =	41:13	X	X	N.P.	X
X	X	41:9b =	41:9b =	41:9b =	41:9c (last half)
41:11 = (last half)	41:14a =	41:10 =	41:10 =	41:10 =	41:10
41:11 = (last half)	41:14b =	41:11 =	41:11 =	41:11 =	41:11
			(reversal	of last half)	
41:12 = (expanded)	41:15 =	41:12 =	41:12 =	41:12 =	41:12
X	X	41:13 =	41:13 =	41:13 =	41:13
X	X	41:14aα	X	N.P.	X
X	X	41:14aβ =	41:14aβ-	41:14a =	41:14a
X	X	41:14b =	41:14b =	41:14b =	41:14bc
X	X	41:15 =	41:15 =	41:15 =	41:15
			(located	here)	
X	X	41:16a =	41:16a =	41:16a =	41:16a
X	X	41:16b =	41:16b =	41:16b =	41:16bc

S^L	S^m	B	M	Y	G^I(Ziegler's)
X	X	41:17 =	41:17 =	41:17 =	41:17
X	X	41:18a =	41:18a =	41:18 =	41:18ab
X	X	41:18b =	41:18b ⎫	41:18c ⎧	41:18c
X	X	41:19a =	41:19a ⎭	⎩	41:19a
X	X	41:19b =	41:19b =	41:19b =	41:19bc
X	X	41:19c =	41:19c =	41:19d =	41:19d
41:12 =	42:1a =	41:20 =	41:20 =	41:20 =	41:20a
41:12 =	42:1b	X	X	N.P.	X
41:12 =	42:2	X	X	N.P.	X
X	X	X	41:20b =	41:20b =	41:20b
X	X	41:21a	41:21a =	41:21ab =	41:21ab
X	X	41:21b =	41:21b =	41:21c =	41:21c

The order and relationships between verses 41:19d - 41:21c:

S^L	S^m	B	M	Y	G^I(Ziegler's)
X	X	41:19c =	41:19c =	41:19d =	41:19d
41:12 =	42:1a =	41:20 =	41:20 ◄─┐	(see below) =	41:20a
41:12	42:1b	X	X	N.P.	X
41:12	42:2	X	X	N.P.	X
X	X	X	41:20b ◄─┤	(see below)	41:20b
X	X	41:21aα	41:21a	41:21a	41:21a
X	X	41:21aβ	41:21a	41:21b	41:21b
				►41:20	
X	X	41:21b	41:21b	41:21c	41:21c
				└►41:20b	
X	X	41:22aβ =	41:22a =	41:22ab =	41:22ab
X	X	41:22b =	41:22b =	41:22cd =	41:22c
X	X	42:1a =	42:1a =	42:1 =	42:1a
X	X	42:1b =	42:1b =	42:1c =	42:1b
X	X	42:1c =	42:1c =	42:1e =	42:1c
X	X	42:2 =	42:2 =	42:2 =	42:2
X	X	42:3 =	42:3 =	42:3 =	42:3
X	X	42:4a =	42:4a =	42:4a,5a =	42:4a
				(= first half of Heb.)	
X	X	42:4b =	42:4b =	42:4bα =	42:4b
X	X	42:5a =	42:5a =	42:4bβ =	42:5a
X	X	X	42:5b =	42:5bc =	42:5b
X	X	42:6 =	42:6 =	42:6 =	42:6
X	X	42:7 =	42:7 =	42:7 =	42:7
X	X	42:8a =	42:8a =	42:8 =	42:8a
X	X	42:8b =	42:8a =	42:8c =	42:8b
42:9 =	42:9a =	42:9a =	42:9a =	42:9 =	42:9a

S^L	S^m	B	M	Y	G^I(Ziegler's)
42:9 =	42:9b =	42:9b =	42:9b =	42:9cd =	42:9b
42:10 =	42:10 =	42:10a =	42:10a =	42:10a =	42:10a
?	?	42:10b =	42:10b =	42:10b =	42:10b
	(perhaps included in 42:10)				
42:11 =	42:11a =	42:11a =	42:11a =	42:11ab =	42:11a
42:11 =	42:11b =	42:11b =	42:11b =	[42:11c] =	42:11b
	(dittography?)				
42:11 =	42:11c =	42:11c =	42:11c =	[42:11e] =	X
42:12 =	42:12 =	42:12 =	42:12 =	[42:12] =	42:12
42:13 =	42:13 =	42:13 =	42:13 =	42:13 =	42:13
X	X	42:14 =	42:14 =	42:14 =	42:14
42:15 =	42:15a =	42:15a =	42:15a =	42:15 =	42:15a
			+	+	
			marg.	marg.	
42:15 =	42:15b =	42:15b =	42:15b =	42:15c =	42:15b
42:16 =	42:16 =	42:16 =	42:16 =	42:16 =	42:16
42:17 =	42:17a =	42:17a =	42:17a =	42:17 =	42:17a
42:17 =	42:17b =	42:17b =	42:17b =	42:17c ~	42:17b
42:18 =	42:18 =	42:18 =	42:18 =	42:18 =	42:18a
42:18,19 =	42:19 =	X =	42:18b =	42:18c =	42:18b
42:19 =	42:20 =	42:19 =	42:19 =	42:19 =	42:19
42:20 =	42:21 =	42:20 =	42:20 =	42:20 =	42:20
42:21 =	42:22 =	42:21a =	42:21a =	42:21 =	42:21a
(= first half of B,M,Y,G^I)					
X	X	42:21b =	42:21b =	42:21c =	42:21b
42:22 =	42:23	X ~	42:22 =	42:22 =	42:22
	(second half altered; some pollution between 22 + 23)				
42:23 =	42:24ab =	42:23 =	42:23 =	42:23 =	42:23
42:23 =	42:24c	X	X	X	X
	(expansion of 24ab)				
42:24 =	42:25a =	42:24 =	42:24 =	[42:24] =	42:24
42:25 =	42:25b =	42:25 =	42:25 =	42:25 =	42:25
X	X	43:1 =	43:1 =	43:1 =	43:1
43:2 =	43:1 =	43:2 =	43:2 =	43:2 =	43:2
	(no verse numbered 43:2)				
43:3 =	43:3 =	43:3 =	43:3 =	43:3 =	43:3
43:4 =	43:4a =	43:4a =	43:4a =	43:4 =	43:4a
43:4 =	43:4b =	43:4b =	43:4b =	[43:4c] =	43:4b
43:5 =	43:5 =	43:5 =	43:5 =	[43:5] =	43:5
43:6 =	43:6 =	43:6 =	43:6 =	[43:6] =	43:6

S^L	S^m	B	M	Y	G^I(Ziegler's)
43:7 =	43:7 =	43:7 =	43:7 =	[43:7] =	43:7
	↑				↑
43:8 =	43:8 =	43:8a ~	43:8a =	[43:8] =	43:8a
	↑				↑
43:8 =	43:9 =	43:8b =	43:8b =	43:8c =	43:8b
43:9 =	43:10 =	43:9 ~	43:9 =	43:9 =	43:9
(= first half of B,M,Y,G^I)					
43:10 =	43:11 =	43:10 =	43:10 =	43:10 =	43:10
	↑				↑
X	X	43:11 =	43:11 =	43:11 =	43:11
X	X	43:12 ~	43:12 =	43:12 =	43:12
X	X	43:13 =	43:13 =	43:13 ~	43:13
X	X	43:14 =	43:14 =	43:14 ~	43:14
X	X	43:15 =	43:15 =	43:15 =	43:15
X	X	43:16ab	{ 43:16a ← → 43:17a { 43:16b ← └→ 43:16a		43:16
X	X	43:17a	43:17aα ⇄ → 43:16b 43:17aβ ← → 43:17b		43:17a
X	X	43:17b = Pattern B–A D–C	43:17b =	43:17cd = Pattern A ＼ ／ C D ／ ＼ B	43:17b
			[Rearrangement makes good sense]		
X	X	43:18 =	43:18 =	43:18 =	43:18
X	X	43:19 =	43:19 =	43:19 =	43:19
X	X	43:20a =	43:20a =	43:20 =	43:20a
X	X	43:20b =	43:20b =	(?43:21ab) =	43:20b
X	X	43:21	...	(?43:21cd) =	43:21
			[Yadin says nothing of 43:21 has survived]		
X	X	43:22	...	[43:22]	43:22
X	X	43:23	...	[43:23]	43:23
X	X	43:24	...	[43:24]	43:24
X	X	43:25	...	[43:25]	43:25
X	X	43:26	X	LOST	43:26
X	X	43:27	X	LOST	43:27
X	X	43:28	X	LOST	43:28
X	X	43:29	X	[43:29]	43:29
X	X	43:30a	X	[43:30a]	43:30a
X	X	43:30b	X	LOST	43:30b
X	X	X	X	LOST	43:31
X	X	43:32	X	LOST	43:32
X	X	43:33	X	LOST	43:33

S^L	S^m	B	M	Y	G^I(Ziegler's)
X	X	44:1a	X	LOST	present-no vs.#
44:1 =	44:1 =	44:1b	...	[44:1] =	44:1
44:2 =	44:2 =	44:2 =	44:2 =	44:2 =	44:2
X	X	44:3a	X	N.P. ~	44:3a
44:3 =	44:3 ~	44:3b =	44:3b =	44:3cd =	44:3b
(inverted)					
44:4 =	44:4 =	44:4a =	44:4a =	44:4 =	44:4ab
X	X	44:4b =	44:4b =	44:4c =	44:4c
44:5 =	44:5 =	44:5 =	44:5 =	44:5 =	44:5
44:6 =	44:6 =	44:6 =	44:6 =	[44:6] =	44:6
44:7 =	44:7 =	44:7 =	44:7 =	[44:7] =	44:7
44:8 =	44:8 =	44:8 =	44:8 =	[44:8] =	44:8
44:9 =	44:9 =	44:9a =	44:9a =	[44:9] =	44:9a
X	X	44:9b =	44:9b =	[44.9c] =	44:9b
44:10 =	44:10 =	44:10 =	44:10 =	[44:10] =	44:10
44:11 =	44:11 ~	44:11 =	44:11 =	44:11 =	44:11
44:12 =	44:12 =	X	44:12 =	44:12 =	44:12
44:13 =	44:13 =	44:13 =	44:13 =	44:13 =	44:13
44:14 =	44:14	... =	44:14 =	44:14 =	44:14
44:15 =	44:15 =	44:15 =	44:15 =	44:15 =	44:15
(second half only)	(added in margin)		(blank line after 44:15		
			indicates new paragraph)		
X	X	44:16	X	N.P.	44:16
44:17 =	44:17,18a =	44:17a =	44:17a =	44:17 =	44:17a
44:17 =	44:18b,19a =	44:17b	...	[44:17c]	44:17b

4
Comparative Translation

Key: B—Ms.B   Key: S—Mosul Syriac
       Bm—margin Ms.B   SL—Vattioni Syriac (Lagarde)
       M—Masada Ms.   G—Ziegler Greek

39:27   B "All ... to the good prove good   thus so for the bad to bad they are turned."
        Bm   to nausea
        M ...   to loathing are turned
39:32   Sm "all these for the good cause good   and for the bad into a curse are turned."
39:27   G "all these to the pious (are) for good   thus for the sinners will be turned into bad."

39:28   B a "There are ...   ... mountains they remove."
        M a   mountains they remove."
39:28c M b " ...   .them they quiet/appease."
39:28a G a "They are winds which were created for
            vengeance   and in their anger they make strong their whips."

39:28–39:30
(39:34–39:36) Syriac

39:28a	G b "In time of consummation they pour out strength	and the anger of the one who created them they calm."
39:33	S a "They are winds that for vengeance were created	and in their anger mountains they destroy."
39:34	S b "And in time of anger their strength they show forth	and the spirit of he who created them they put at rest."
39:29	B "Fire and hail, misfortune and pestilence	also these for judgment were created.
	M "...	... were created."
39:29	G "Fire and hail and famine and death	all these for vengeance were created,"
39:35	S "Fire and hail and stones (?) (of) death	all these for judgment were created."
39:30	B "Beast of tooth/beast of prey, scorpion and snake	and sword of vengeance to destroy ..."
	Bm	...bm
	M	
	G "of beasts' teeth, and scorpions and vipers	and a scimitar bringing vengeance for the ruin of the ungodly."

39:30–39:31
(39:35–39:37) Syriac

39:36	S "beasts of teeth and scorpions and snakes	the sword of punishment to destroy the wicked."
39:30bc	B "all these for their use were created	and they (are) in supply and for the time they will be summoned."
	Bm were chosen	in his supply for the time
	M "...	his
39:30		...
39:31	G a "in his command they will be happy	b and upon the earth they will be made ready
		c and in their times they will not transgress a word."
39:37	S "In the time that he summons them they rejoice	and in all their days they will not transgress his word."
	SL	and all their days they will not transgress
39:31	B "when he commands them, they rejoice	and in their prescribed task they do not disobey his word."
	Bm	
	M	

39:32–39:34
(39:38–39:40) Syriac

39:32	B	"Therefore from the beginning I stood assured	and I considered (it) and in writing I set it down."
	M	"...	...y
39:32	G	"Because of this from the beginning I was fixed/determined	and I thought it over and in writing I left it."
39:38	S	"Because from the beginning they were created	understand O men! that in a book all these are written."
39:33	B	"The work ? of God, all of them are good, all	for every use in its time it is sufficient. use
	Bm		
39:33	G	"The works of the Lord are all good	and every need in its hour he will supply."
39:39	S	"and all his works are good	and every thing for its time was created."
39:34	B	"One should not say 'this is worse than that,' than that	for everything in its time prevails/is strong." prevails
	Bm	not	
39:34	G	"and one should not say 'this is worse than that'	for everything in time will be useful."

39:35–40:1ab
(39:40–40:1ab) Syriac

39:40	S "one should not say 'this is worse than that,'	because all things are gathered in storehouses and in due season prove useful."
39:35	B "Now with all the heart and mouth, cry-for-joy	praise the name of the Holy One."
	Bm	His holiness
39:35	G "and now with all the heart and mouth sing praise	and bless the name of the Lord."
39:41	S "Therefore with all your heart, bless God	and praise his name."
40:1a	B "Great trouble God apportioned	and a heavy yoke upon the sons of men."
	Bm	Elyon
40:1b	B "from the day of his going forth from the womb of his mother	to the day of his returning to the mother of all life."
	Bm	God of all life
40:1a	G "Great trouble/labor was created for every man	and a heavy yoke upon the sons of Adam."
40:1b	G "from the day of going forth from the belly of their mother	to the day of return to the mother of all."

40:2(GS)–40:4
(40:2–40:3a) Syriac

40:1a	S "God created many things	and strong manners/ways upon the sons of men."
40:1b	S "from the day they came forth from the womb of their mother	until they recline/return to the land of the living."
40:2	G "Their disputations and fear of heart	anxious thought, a day of finality."
40:2	S "Their belief and the thought of their heart	the direction of their words, to the day of death."
40:3	B "from him who sits (on) the throne exalted	returning (to) dust and ashes."
Bm	he who sits	to the one clothed
40:3	G "from the one sitting on a glorious throne	and to the one who is humbled in dirt and ashes."
40:3	S "from those who sit (upon) the thrones of kings	to those who sit (in) dust and ash."
40:4	B "from the one wearing turban and ornament	to the one wearing (his) sleeping mat."
Bm		to the one wearing
40:4	G "from him who wears purple and crown	and to the one wrapped (in) burlap."
40:3a	S "from those who wear the crown	to those who wear the garment of poverty."

40:5a–40:6b

(40:3b–40:5,6a) Syriac

40:5a	B	"Indeed (there are) jealousy, anxiety and fear	and fear of death, strife ...
	Bm		death, ?, contention
40:5a	G	"anger and envy and disorder and disturbance	and fear of death and fury and strife."
40:3b	S	"anger and grief and jealousy	and fear of death and dispute and quarreling."
	SL	"anger and grief and jealousy and fear"	
40:5b	B	"And (at the) time of his resting upon his bed	the sleep of the night is disturbed..."
	Bm		"doubles his unhappiness"
40:5b	G	"and in the time of resting upon a bed	the sleep of night alters his knowledge."
40:5,6a	S	"and in the time of resting upon their beds	in the sleep of the night it awakens them."
40:6b	B	"A little idle time, for a moment he may rest	and from an interval in dreams
	Bm		
40:6b	B	"A little deceived by the vision of his soul	like a refugee in.. ... the pursuer."

40:6a–40:8
(40.6b–40:7) Syriac

40:6a	G "A little, like none, in rest	and from that in sleep(s) as in a restless day
40:6b	G disturbed by a vision of his heart/mind	as one having escaped from battle-front."
40:6b	S "He deliberates in a vision of the night	like a man who escapes from before the persecutor.
40:7	B Smend: "Again needing sleep he awakens	and blind fright has robbed his slumber."
40:7	G "at the time of his need he is awakened	marvels (that) fear (came) to nothing,"
40:7	S "if pleasure is in his heart he watches	and sees that there is nothing there."
	SL as, as if	
40:8	B ...	...
	Bm "with all f(lesh)...	also with ..."
	M ...	....ym k'lh
40:8	G "with all flesh from man to beast	and upon sinners 7 times (more) than these;

40:8–40:11

(40:8–40:11) Syriac

40:8	S "with all the sons of flesh their anxiety is with them"	riches disturb their sleep."
40:9	B "Pestilence and bloodshed, fever and sword"	devastation and destruction, evil and death/plague."
40:9	G "death and bloodshed and strife and sword"	calamities, famine and affliction and scourge/plague."
40:10	B "for the wicked was created evil"	and on (his) account annihilation departs (Smend: "does not depart")
	Bm	same
	Bmm	same
40:10	G "for the lawless was created all these things"	and because of them the flood came."
40:11	B "all from the earth to the earth will return"	and that which is from "on high" to "on high."
	Bm	שׁוּב
	M "all from.. ..."	...

40:11–40:13
(40:11–40:13) Syriac

40:11	G "all things which are from the earth, to the earth return	and from the waters, to the sea goes back.
40:11	S "everything that from the earth is, to the earth returns	and that from on high to on high."
40:12	M "all (that is from)... ...	...
40:12	G "all bribery and injustice will be wiped out	but faithfulness will stand for ever"
40:12	S "anyone who sins and lies will come to an end	but the eternally faithful will likewise stand."
40:13	B חיל אל כחול like a raging torrent	and from a water-course mighty in a thunderstorm."
	Bm חיל כחול	
	M חיל מעול "wealth from iniquity"	אומיק)
		.t
40:13	G "The possessions of the unjust as a river will be dried up	and like loud thunder in rain it will sound."
40:13	S "The possessions of falsehood like a torrent will be swept away	and like rivers that are filled (melên) from fleeting rainclouds."

40:14–40:15
(40:14a–40:15a) Syriac

40:14

B "As it rises up rocks ילגי
Bm עם שאנו
(Yadin ילגנ "are rolled away"
(Smend ילגי "roll away")

M "As it rises up ro(cks)...

for suddenly forever it comes to an end."

40:14 G "When he opens his hands he will be made glad

...

40:14a S "when they are deprived (g-l-z)

likewise transgressors will ultimately pass away."

they will be finished off, and a change for wicked men will not be."

40:15

B "A sprout from violence will not take root
Bm "A sprout-of violence will not ?
M "A sprout-of violence will not .. ...

for an impious root (is) on the ledge of a cliff.
for an impious root (is) ? the ledge of a rock.
... upon ... rock

40:15 G "The children of the ungodly will not put forth shoots

40:15a S "For the root of sinners is like the ear-of-wheat that sprouts upon a rocky crag."

for unhealthy roots (are they) upon sharp rock."

40:16–40:17
(40:15b–40:17a) Syriac

40:16	B	"like קדמת upon the bank-of a wadi	from before all rain are dried up."
	Bm		
40:16	M	"like reed-stalks upon the banks of a wadi	... green grass is dried up."
40:15b	G	"reeds upon any water or river bank	before any feed/grass will be plucked."
	S	"and like bindweed that sprouts upon the bank of a wadi	before any herb it dries up."
40:17	B	"and mercy forever will not be moved	righteousness for ever will be firm."
	M	"mercy like eternity, will not be cut off	and righteousness for ever will be firm."
40:17	G	"kindness/graciousness is like a garden with blessings	and mercy forever will endure."
40:17a	S	"the works of the just in time are blessed	and the works of the righteous forever will stand."

40:18–40:18
(40:17b–40:18) Syriac

40:18	B	"A life-of wine and beer is sweet	but (better than) them both is he who finds a treasure,"
	Bm	חיי יין ושכר	מטמון
40:18	M	"A life-of luxury (and) remuneration is sweet	but (better than) them both is he who finds ..."
	G	"Life of-self-sufficiency and of-work will be sweet	but better than both is he who finds a treasure,
40:17b	S	"it comes (near) to them like a man who finds a treasure,"	

40:19a	B	"A child and a city establish a name	but (better than) them both is he who finds wisdom."
	M	"A child and.. (est)ablish a name	but (better than) them both is he who finds ..."
40:19	G	"Children and the building of a city establish a name	but a blameless wife is considered above both,"
40:18	S	"Greatness and honor est. a name	but better than the two of them is he who finds wisdom."

40:19b–40:21
(40:19–40:21) Syriac

40:19b	B	"offspring and a plantation make a name flourish	but (better than) them both is a devoted wife."
	M	שאר	
	G		
40:19	S	"a building and a planatation dedicate a name	but (better than) them both is a wise wife."
40:20	B	"wine and beer rejoice the heart	but better than them both is the love of friends."
40:20	G	"wine and music rejoice the heart	but better than both is the love of wisdom.
40:20	S	"old wine gladdens the heart	but better than it is the love of a friend.
40:21	B	"the flute and harp make a song pleasing	but better than the two of them is a healthy voice."
	Bm	דדלל	
40:21	G	"flute and harp sweeten a melody	but better than both is pleasant voice."
40:21	S	"flute and harp make a song pleasant	but better than both (is) a pure voice"

40:22–40:24
(40:22–40:23) Syriac

40:22	B ... make the eye notice Bm	but better than both are sprouts of the field." שדי
40:22	G "The eye desires grace and beauty	but better than both is the green-blade of the seed"
40:22	S "loveliness and beauty (is) the desire of the eyes	but better than them both are the ears (of wheat) of the field."
40:23	B ... .t יהדו	but better than both (is) a prudent wife.
40:23	G "A friend and companion appear at the right time	but better than both (is) a woman with (her) husband.
40:23	S "A friend and companion at (the right) time bring a blessing	but better than both is a good wife."
40:24	B "A brother ... distress Bm	but better than both justice delivers."
40:24	G "Brothers and help are for a time of trouble	but better than both mercy delivers."

40:25–40:26b
(40:24–40:26) Syriac

40:24	S "A brother and a helper (are) for a time of affliction	but better than both alms redeem."
40:25	B "Gold and silver l	but better than both..."
40:25	G "Gold and silver will make the foot stand sure	but better than both counsel is esteemed."
40:25	S "Gold and silver make the foot stand	but better than both (is) good advice."
40:26b	B "power and strength (rejoice) the heart	but better than both is the fear of God."
	M ...שירה...	
40:26a	G "Possessions and strength will lift up the heart	but above both is the fear of the Lord."
40:26	S "strength and power lift up the heart	but better than both is the fear of God."
40:26b	B "There is not in the fear of YYY want	and not need to seek with it support."
	M ... loss	and not need to seek with it support."
	G "There is not in the fear of the Lord	and no need to seek with it help."

40:27–40:29a
(40:27–40:29) Syriac

40:27	S "There is not in the fear of God lack	and not need to seek with it help."
40:28	S "The fear of God over everything is exalted; seize it, my son, and do not slacken because there is nothing like it."	
40:27	B "The fear of God is like an Eden of blessing	and thus all honor (is) (its) canopy."
	M ...	and over all that is glorious (is) (its) canopy."
40:27	G "The fear the Lord is like a paradise of blessing	and better than all glory it covered him."
40:28b	S "the fear of God in time brings a blessing	and above all honor it is glorified."
40:28	B MNY the life of gift do not live	better is one gathered/dead than behaving haughtily."
	Bm "my son	
	M ...	better is one dead than impudent."
40:28	G "Child, the life of begging do not live	it is better to die than to beg."
40:29	S "My son, whoever begs you, do not refuse him	you will not do good to kill, rather it is good only to cause life."
40:29a	B "A man who gazes upon the table of a stranger	not his life to be counted as life."

40:29a–40:30
(40:30–40:31) Syriac

M

40:29a	G	"A man looking to the table belonging to another	his life is not in an accounting of life,
40:30	S	"A man who hopes upon the table of others	no one considers him to be alive,"
40:29b	B	"A pollution of the soul (are) his dainties	to the man who knows private inner parts,"
	Bm	"A pollution of his soul are dainties of endowment dainties	to the man who departs from (מעים)
	M	...	to the man who knows discipline of inward parts."
40:29b	G	"he will pollute his soul with foods which belong-to-others	but a prudent man and instructed will guard himself."
	S	? ↳	
40:31	S	"his soul hates whoever desires pleasures	but to the man who knows these things, pain they are of the intestines."
40:30	B	"to the man bold of soul, begging tastes sweet	but inside of him it burns like fire"

40:30–41:1b
(40:32–41:1) Syriac

Bm בכמרה עד נבשה   באש במרחה

    M "in the mouth of a bold man t..."   ... him like fire it burns."

40:30   G "in the mouth of the shameless begging turns sweet but in his intestines a fire will be set on fire."

40:32   S "in the mouth of the shameless sweet is his begging but like fire it burns inside him."

41:1a   B "Hail to death, how bitter does he bless   to the man living-at-peace at his habitation."

Bm הוי

    M "h.. l.. ... (is) your remembrance

41:1a   G "O death, how piercingly bitter is your reminder   to the man living-at-peace at his habitation."

41:1   S "O death, how bad you are   to a man dwelling peacefully among his belongings."
     to the rich man who dwells upon his goods."

41:1b   B "A man at ease and successful in everything   and still in him strength to receive pleasure."

    M ... at ease and successful in everything   still in him strength to receive pleasure."

41:1b–41:2b
(41:2–41:3) Syriac

41:1b   G "to the man undistracted and having free course in
        all things   and still with strength to receive pleasure."

41:2   S "to the man who is strong and successful at all
        times   and yet there is in him strength to receive delicacies."

41:2a   B "Ah to death, for good is your decree
        חזק or חזיק or חיזק   to the man power and lacking strength."

Bm
M   "... ' to death how good...

41:2a   G "O death, good is your judgment   to the one without power and lacking strength."
41:3   S "O death, how welcome you are   to the man failing and diminishing in strength."
                                                  to the man who is broken and lacks vitality."

41:2b   B "A man stumbling and striking against everything   discontented and void-of hope."
Bm¹ ונגש
Bm²   "A man stumbling and trapped by everything   without sight and void-of hope."
Bm³   "A man trapped and ונגש by everything   without sight and void-of hope."
M   "A man stumbling and trapped by...   without sight and void-of hope."

4::2b–41:4a
(41:5–41:6) Syriac

41:2b	G "to the old man and distracted over everything	to the disagreeable man and without patience."
41:4	S "An old man who stumbles all the time	and lacks sustenance and there is not in him strength to work."

SL

mmwn for *mzwn*

41:3	B "do not fear death, your decree	remember that first and last (are) with you."
	M "do not fear death, your decree	remember first and last are with you."
41:3	G "do not fear the judgment of death	remember your former/predecessors and latter."
41:5	S "do not fear death because it is your lot	remember those of former and latter are with you."

41:4a	B "this is the lot of all flesh from God	and how can you avert the law of the most high?"
	M "this is the end of all ...	most high?"
41:4a	G "this is the judgment from the Lord for all flesh	and how can you reject the will of the most high?"
41:6	S "because this is the end of all men before God."	

41:4b–41:5
(41:8) Syriac

41:4b

B "for a thousand years, a hundred, or ten   a man reproaches in Sheol (regarding) life."
Bm
M "for ten, a hundred or a thousand years   there are no

41:4b

G "whether ten, a hundred or a thousand years   there is not in Hades disputation (regarding) life."
S no verse   ...

41:5

B "an offspring rejected is the דבר of the evil   and a foolish sprout the ... of the wicked."
Bm מי   עולם
M "an offspring rejected are the generations of the evil

41:5

G "disgusting children the children of sinners become   and they associate in the houses of the ungodly."

41:8

S "an abominable seed (is) the generation of sinners   and the family—woe to it; the generation of the iniquitous."
SL   the sinners   ...   wicked."

ᶜ1:6–41:8
(41:9–41:10) Syriac

41:6   B "From the son-of an evil-doer dominion-oᵓ bad/broken   ... his seed ..."
       Bm מבן לרע   ܠܫܙ
       M " ... ..l dominion perishes   ... always contempt."

41:6   G "the inheritance of the children of sinners will perish   and with their seed will always be reproved."

41:9   S "From a lawless son dominion perishes   and with his seed will dwell need."

41:7   B "a wicked father a child will curse   for ..ll.. ..."
       M ...   will curse   ... (on) his account they have contempt."

41:7   G "children will blame an ungodly father   because on his account they will be reproached."

41:10   S "a lawless father, his upright sons will curse him   for because of him they were reduced in the world."
       sL   *bsyr'*

41:8   B " ... ..l.. ...   ...wn
       M " ... men of evil-doing   who forsake the laws of the most high."

41:8–41:9ab
(41:11–41:13) Syriac

41:8   G "woe to you, ungodly men,   who forsake the laws of the most high."
41:11   S "woe to them, lawless men   for sickness accompanies them until the day of their
                                              death."

41:9a   B "if … … hands-of an accident   … offspring for sighing."
        Bm¹ "   you are fruitful
        Bm² "if you are fruitful upon/by accident   and if you have offspring for sighing,"
        M … .l…   and if you have offspring (?) for sighing."
41:9ab G "For, if you prevail, for destruction   and if you are born, for a curse you will be born."
        S

41:12   S "A fertile woman (is) for the joy of her people,"
41:13   S "But if a lawless father dies, his upright sons will not mourn over him."

41:9b–41:10
(41 14a) Syriac

41:9b

B "if you stumble—for everlasting joy"   and if you die—for a curse."

Bm   להללבה

M "... .w—for everlasting joy"   and if you die—for a curse."

G

S   "and if you die—you will be allotted a curse."

41:9c

G

S

41:10

B "all (that is) from nothing to nothing will return   thus the ungodly from nothing to nothing."

Bm¹   from powers/evils to powers/evils

Bm² "all (that is) from powers/evils to powers/evils

Bm³   מן

M "... .. nothing to nothing will return   thus the ungodly from nothing to nothing."

G "all things that are from the earth will to the earth go

41:10

S   thus the ungodly from curse to destruction."

41:14a

S   for the wicked, his end is destruction."

41:11–41:12
(41:14b–41:15) Syriac

41:11	B "vain (is) man in his body	but a kind name will not be cut off."
	Bm בני	
	M " ..l ...	... a kind name will not be cut off."
41:11	G "the mourning of men is in their bodies	and the un-good name of sinners will be blotted out."
41:14b	S	but the name of the workers-of good things will not ever be lost."
41:12	B "fear for a name, for it will accompany you	more than thousands of stores-of wisdom."
	Bm¹	מטמני
	Bm²	חכמה
	M "fear for a name for it will accompany you	more than thousands of ..."
	G "have regard for your name for it will remain with you	
41:12	S "fear for your name for it will accompany you	more than a thousand great stores of gold."
41:15		more than a thousand treasures of temporal nature

41:13–41:14a

(41:13–21b not in Syriac)

41:15	S	because gifts and treaties perish"
41:13	B	"The good things of life (have) days-of number ⎯ but the good things of a name (have) days of no number."
	Bm¹	"The good-of life (has) numbered days
	Bm²	מספר
41:13	M	"The good-things of life (have) numbered days ⎯ but the good-things ... no number."
	G	"(regarding) a good life (its) days are numbered ⎯ but a good name abides forever."
	S	
41:14a	B	"an exhortation (of) shame/discretion is a name," ⎯ ? instruction (with) discretion ... "an exhortation (of) shame."
41:14a	B	"instruction (with) discretion hear, children"
41:14a	M	"instruction (with) discretion hear, children"

41:14a–41:16a

41:14a	G "receive instruction peacefully, children."	
41:14b	B "hidden wisdom and concealed treasure חכמה מטמונת	what use is there in either of them?" תעלה
Bm		
	M "hidden wisdom and concealed treasure	what use is there in either of them?"
41:14bc	G "hidden wisdom and an unseen treasure	what use (is there) in both?"
41:15	B "better is the man hiding his foolishness	than the man hiding his wisdom."
Bm		מאיש מטמין
	M "better is the man hiding his foolishness	than the man hiding his wisdom."
41:15	G "better is the man hiding his foolishness	than the man hiding his wisdom."
41:16a	B "and be humble concerning my judgment" his	
Bm		
	M "and be humble concerning my judgment"	

41:16a–41:17

41:16a G "therefore show respect regarding my judgment,"

41:16b B "for not every shame is fitting to observe   and not all humiliation choice."
C same
M "for not every shame is fitting to be ashamed of   and not all humiliation choice."

41:16bc G "for it is not good to keep every kind of shame   and not everything by all in confidence is held in esteem."

41:17 B "be ashamed of a father and mother to wantonness from a prince who dwells to/on falsehood."
Bm   עַל פֶּתַה
Bm regarding wantonness   עַל יֹשֵׁר
   and a ruler regarding
M "be ashamed of a father and mother to wantonness from a prince who dwells to/on falsehood."
G "be ashamed of a father and mother concerning fornication   and of a prince or authority concerning a lie"

41:18a–41:19a

41:18a   B "of a master and mistress of the lie   from an assembly and a people of transgression."

41:18a   M "of a master and mistress of the lie   from an assembly and a people of transgression."

41:18ab   G "of a judge and a ruler regarding an error   from a congregation and a people regarding lawlessness."

41:18b   B "from a friend and companion concerning betrayal

41:18b   M "from a friend and companion concerning betrayal

41:18c   G "from a companion and friend concerning injustice

41:19a   B "and from a place (where) you live regarding the illicit:

       Bm " and a leader regarding power

41:19a   M "and from a place (where) you live regarding power."

41:19a   G "and from a place where you live, regarding theft."

41:19b–41:20a

41:19b	B "... oath or covenant	from stretching the elbow for bread."
	M "from breaking oath or covenant	and from stretching the elbow for bread."
41:19bc	G "from the truth of God and a covenant	and from fixing of the elbow at bread(s)."
41:19c	B "... a request"	
	Bm "mm.. to grant a request"	
	M "from withholding to grant a request"	
41:19d	G "from contemptuous-treatment regarding receiving and giving,"	
41:20	B ..ly peace from keeping silent"	
	Bm from one who greets keeping silent"	
	Bm "from the greeting be silent"	
	M "from him who greets, keep silent"	
41:20a	G "and from those who greet regarding silence"	
42:1	S "all who inquire regarding his welfare and (he remains) silent	and that one is a great robber."

41:20b–41:21b
(42:2–) Syriac

42:2   S "A (greeting) that you give him, he will not answer you; a deposit that you give him, how will he return (it) to you?"

41:20b   M "and from looking to a strange woman"
41:20b   G "from looking at a strange woman"

41:21a   B "from turning away the face of your friend   from turning away the share-of a portion."
    Bm¹ "who will deliver the mouth"
    Bm² "who will deliver the mouth-of your friend   from the reckoning of the share-of a portion."
    M "and from turning away the face-of your kinsman   from stopping   the share-of a portion."
41:21ab   G "and from turning away the face of a kinsman   from taking away a portion or gift."

41:21b   B "from looking upon .. ..
    Bm   אשר

41:21c–42:1a

41:21c
M "from looking upon .. ..."
G "from observing a married woman."

41:22a
B
Bm "
and from vi(olating) .. l ...
ה..

41:22a   M "from being-intimate with your maid-servant   and from violating upon her bed."
41:22ab G "from meddling with his maidservant   and do not set upon her marriage-bed,"

41:22b   B "from a friend concerning (..y) reproach   and after giving do not (treat with contempt.)"
Bm   a word-of shame   a request
         M "from a friend concerning words of shame   and from after giving, reproach."
41:22   G "from friends concerning words-of reproach   and after giving, do not reproach,"

42:1a   B "from repeating a word you hear   and from laying bare every private counsel."

42:1a–42:2

			על אמר
	Bm		
42:1a	M	"from repeating a word you hear	and from laying bare every word-of-counsel."
	G	"from repetition of a word heard	and from revelation of hidden words."
42:1b	B	"and you will be ashamed truly	and find favor in the eyes-of all living."
42:1b	M	"and you (will) be ashamed truly	and find favor in the eyes-of all living,"
42:1b	G	"and you will be ashamed truly	and find favor with every man."
42:1c	B	"but concerning these do not be ashamed	and do not lift up faces and sin."
	Bm		אל
42:1c	M	"... concerning these do not be ashamed	and do not lift up faces and sin."
42:1c	G	"not concerning these be ashamed	and do not receive a face to sin."
42:2	B	"concerning the law of the most high and the statute	and concerning justice to justify the wicked."
	Bm	אל	במשפט

42:3–42:4

    M "concerning the law of the most high and the statute"   concerning justice to justify the wicked."

    G "concerning the law of the most high and the covenant"   and concerning judgment to acquit the ungodly."

רשע

42:3´   B "concerning reckoning with a friend and master"   and concerning division of inheritance and property."

    Bm   ואדה שמו

42:3   M "concerning reckoning (with) a friend and traveller"   and concerning division of inheritance and property."

    G "concerning reasoning with a friend and traveller"   and concerning distributing the inheritance of others."

42:4a   B "and concerning the dust-of the scales and the balance"   and of cleaning of measure and weight."

    Bm   exchanging ephah or ephah

    M "concerning the dusts-of the scales and the balance"   and of cleanings-of measure and weight."

42:4   G "concerning exactness of scales and weights"   and of acquisition of much or little."

42:4b–42:6

42:4b
B "concerning buying between much or little
Bm   reckoning
M "concerning buying between much or little

42:5a
B "and concerning purchasing in trading (with) a merchant."
Bm מוכר
M "... bargaining in trading (with) a merchant."

42:5b
M "... ..h   and a bad servant and one who limps (in) walking."

42:5
G "and of profit-making in selling (with) merchants
"and of much instruction of children   and to a bad servant making the side bleed."

42:6
B "on a bad wife a seal (is) wise   and a place of weak hands you will lock."
Bm מפתח
Bm "on a bad wife a seal   and a place of weak hands you will lock."
M ...   putting a seal   and a place of many hands a key."

42:6–42:8b

42:6	G "upon a bad wife good is a sacrificial knife	and where hands are many lock up."
42:7	B "upon a place (where) you deposit you will write a number	and giving and taking—all in writing."
	Bm במקום יד תחשב	and asking and giving
	M "upon... you deposit—a number	š.. and giving—all in writing."
42:7	G "whatever you give-in number and weight	and giving and taking—all in writing,"
42:8a	B "concerning the correction of the simple and stupid	and the old and senile and he who lifts/takes counsel in whoredom."
	Bm מדרה	
	Bm	and the old and stumbling and occupied with whoredom."
42:8a	M "concerning m.. of the simple & stupid	the old and stumbling occupied with whoredom."
	G "concerning instruction of the stupid and foolish	and of the old judging concerning fornication;"
42:8b	B "and you will be warned truly	and a man modest before all living."
	M "and you will be warned truly	before all living,"
		...

42:8b–42:9b
(42:9a–42:9b) Syriac

42:8b	G "and you will be instructed truly	and approved before all living."
42:9a	B "A daughter to a father is a hidden-treasure of deception	and worry tp.. ..."
	Bm מכמן	
	M "a b... to a father is a hidden-treasure š..	... ..yd rest." ואבתה
42:9a	G "a daughter to a father is hidden sleeplessness	and anxiety over her disturbs his sleep."
42:9a	S "a daughter upon her father is a heavy burden	and anxiety over her disturbs his sleep."
42:9b	B "in her youth lest she commit adultery	and in her young-womanhood lest..."
	M "in her youth lest she be hated/rejected	and in her... lest...
42:9b	G "in her youth lest she pass her prime	and married lest she be hated/rejected."
42:9b	S "in her youth lest she be disgraced	and in her prime years lest she be hated."

42:10a–42:10b
(42:10–) Syriac

42:10a

B "In her young-womanhood lest she תחמה — and in the house ..L. l.. ...
Bm¹ תחמה
Bm² "In her young-womanhood lest תחמה — .. house of master/husband l.. forgotten."
Bm³

M "In her young-womanhood lest she be defiled — and upon her husband she turns aside."
G "in virginity, lest she be profaned — and in her father's house she became pregnant."
S "in her virginity lest she devise plans — and upon her husband lest she be unfaithful in her mind and go after another man."

42:10b

B " in the house-of her father lest... — and in the house-of her husband...she be barren."
Bm¹ father she be loose
Bm²,³ in the house-of her father p... — and in the house-of her husband lest she be barren."
M "house-of her father lest she bear seed — and in her husband's ..."
G "being with her husband, lest she go astray — and being married, lest she be barren."

42:11a	S included in 42:10		
	B " ... .l ... .l. ... watch		... name of rebellion"
	Bm		corruption"
	Bm	בן על כם חזק פן תשמח בת מועצת כי לא	lest t... ..."
42:11a	M " ... concerning a daughter (keep) careful watch		
	G "over a headstrong daughter make strong (your) guard		lest she make you a laughing stock to (your) enemies."
42:11a	S "my son, over your daughter keep watch		lest she make you a bad name"
42:11b	B "the gossip-of the city and the congregation of the people		and she make you sit ..(in) the assembly of the gate."
			והתביש[ן
	Bm¹		
	Bm² "the gossip of the city and the congregation of the people		and she shame (you) in the assembly of the gate."
	M "the gossip-of the city and the congregation of the people		...
42:11b	G "gossip in the city and noticed/chosen by the people		and she shame you in a crowd of many."
42	S "the talk and murmuring among the people		{ in the murmuring of the people"
			{ in the assembly of your city she shame you,

42:11c–42:13
(42:11c–42:12) Syriac

42:11c

B "the place where she dwells, let there not be a window — or a place overlooking the entrance surrounding."

Bm שׁו(ת)

M "the place where she dwells, let there not be... — ... ..b

G

42:11c

S "the place where she dwells, let her not leave it by going out — and in houses let her not be wandering.

42:12

B "to every male let her not give (her) figure — and (in) the house of women let her not converse

Bm ...zkr.

M "to every male let her not reveal (her) figure

42:12

G "to every person do not look for beauty — "..."

S "to every man do not reveal what is in your heart — and in the midst of women do not sit together." — and among women do-not-make-frivolous chatter."

42:13

B "for from a garment goes forth moth — and from woman the evil of women."

42:13–42:15a

(42:13–42:15a) Syriac

			Syriac
42:13	M	"for from a garment goes forth moth"	..h the evil of woman."
42:13	G	"for from garments goes forth moth"	and from woman the evil of woman."
42:13	S	"for as in a garment there falls a moth"	thus jealousy in a wife/woman from the badness of her female companion."
42:14	B	"better is the badness of a man than the goodness of a woman"	and the daughter who reproaches אשה הרע מבית
	Bm¹,²	מטוב רע אשה מטוב	
42:14	M	better is the badness of a man than the goodness of a woman	ובת מחפרת מבית הרע
42:14	G	"better the evil of a man than the doing-good woman"	the daughter מפחדת from all reproach.
	S		and a woman brings shame unto disgrace."
42:15a	B	"I will now recall the works of God"	and what I have seen also I will recount."
42:15a	M	"I will now recall the works of God"	and what I have seen also I will repeat."
	Bm	"I will now recall my works"	and what I have seen also I will repeat."
42:15a	G	"I will now recall the works of the Lord"	and what I have seen I will tell in detail."
42:15a	S	"remember there are the works-of God"	and from what I have seen I will repeat;

42:15b–42:17a
(42:15a–42:16) Syriac

	42:15b		
42:15b	B	"by the word-of God – his will מעשיו	and the work-of his will – his teaching."
	Bm		
42:15b	M	"by the word-of the Lord – his works	and the work-of his will – his teaching." לקח
42:15b	G	"by the words of the Lord – his works	and with his approval judgment has come."
42:15b	S	"by his word his works were created	and these, his creatures, his will are doing."
42:16	B	"the sun shining over all that is revealed	and the glory of YYY over all his works."
42:16	M	"the sun shining over all that is (revealed)	and the glory of 'dny (fills) his works."
42:16	G	"the sun shining on all it looked upon	and his work full of the glory of the Lord."
42:16	S	"as the sun that is manifested upon all	the mercies of the Lord upon all his works are revealed."
42:17a	B	"They are not sufficient, the holy ones of God	to recount the miracles of YYY. mighty deeds
	Bm		

42:17a–42:18a
(42:17a–42:18) Syriac

42:17a   M "They are not sufficient, the holy ones of God   to recount all his miracles.

     G "He did not put-it-out to the holy ones of the Lord to declare all his marvels,"

42:17a   S "the holy ones of the Lord are not able   to recount the greatness of his miracles;"

42:17b   B "God strengthened his hosts   to be strong before his glory."

     Bm   אמץ   לההרין

     M "the Lord strengthened his hosts   to be strong before his glory."

42:17b   G "which the Almighty Lord established   that everything/the universe may be firm in his glory."

42:17b   S "he gave strength to those who fear him   to stand before his glory."

42:18   B "the deep and the heart he searches out   and into all their secrets he examines."

     M "the deep and the heart he searches out   and into their secrets he examines."

42:18a   G "the abyss and heart he traced out   and into their crafty-plans he thought over;"

42:18   S "the deep and the heart he explores   and all the hidden-things of men, as the sun, are revealed before him."

42:18b–42:20
(42:19–42:20) Syriac

42:18b	M "for knowledge is to 'ELYON all...	and seeing what comes (upon) the world/eternity."
42:18b	G "for MOST HIGH knew all to know	and looked into the sign of the age/eternity."
42:19	S "because nothing is hidden from God	and there appear before him all that comes to the world."
42:19	B "declaring what-has-passed (and) what-will-occur	and revealing deep hidden-things."
Bm	ונהיות	
42:19	M "declaring what-has-passed (and) ...	and revealing deep hidden-things."
42:19	G "declaring the things passed and the things coming	and revealing the tracks of hidden things."
42:20	S "that which has passed and that which will happen	and all things hidden are revealed before him."
42:20	B "Not lacking from him (is) all insight	and no matter passes him."
Bm	הלא דבר כל דבר	
42:20	M "Not lacking from before him is insight	and no matter passes him."

42:20–42:22
(42:21–42:21b) Syriac

42:20   G "No thought passes him   and not one word is hidden from him."

42:21   S "not lacking from before him (is) all wisdom   and no great secret hides from before him."

42:21a   B "g.. .tw is established   one is HE from everlasting."
Bm בכבודה
M "the might of his wisdom...   מעולם

42:21a   G "the great-things of his wisdom he arranged   one HE is from everlasting to everlasting."
S

42:21b   B l. ... and nothing taken away   and he does not need any counsel."
Bm   צריך
M "nothing added ...   and not ... deny counsel."

42:21b   G "nothing was added nothing taken away   he has no need of anyone's counsel."
S

42:22   M "are not all his works lovely?   unto a spark or visions-of (its) appearance."

42:22–42:24
(42:22–42:24) Syriac

42:22	B	
	G "as all his works (are) desirable	and as of a spark they are to behold."
	S	
42:23	B "he... forever	and to every need ... he will respond/hear."
	Bm "and abides"	for every need everything is heard."
	M "everything lives and stands forever	in every need all is kept.
42:23	G "all these-things live and abide forever	and for all needs, also all respond.
42:22	S "and wisdom stands before him forever	
42:23	S "and all his works forever truly he establishes	and with holiness all of them praise"
42:24	S "and they live and stand forever	and for all of them all his will(s) are prepared."
		and they hasten in deed in their power/influence"
42:24	B "all of them by two's, one opposite the other	and he did not make from them vanity/uselessness"

42:24–42:25b
(42:25a–42:25b) Syriac

42:24	M "all of them ... side-by-side with the other	did not make from them...
	G "all-things twofold, one opposite the other	and he did not make anything incomplete."
42:25a	S "all of them two by two, one opposite the other	and he did not create one of them uselessly."
42:24	B "one with another exchanges its good	and who can be satisfied l.. ..."
	Bm "one with another exchanges twb..	and who can be satisfied to behold (their) form?"
	M "one with another exchanges their good	and who can be satisfied to behold their splendor
42:25	G "one confirms/strengthens the good-things of the other	and who will be filled of beholding his glory?"
42:25b	S "only this (one) with that, in couples	and who can be satisfied to behold their glory?"
43:1	B ... for purity	and the firm heaven *mrbyt* its splendor."
	Bm "the beauty of the height and firmament on purity	and the firm heaven beholds (its) light."

43:1–43:3
(43:1–43:1) Syriac

43:1	M "the beauty of the height and firmament for purity	the firm heaven m.. ...rw"
	G "the pride of the height is the clear firmament	the appearance of heaven in a view of glory."
	S	
43:2	B "the sun pours forth in its scorching warmth	what wonders the words of YYY.
	Bm shines forth in its going forth	
43:2	M "the sun shines forth in its going forth fulness	instruments of wonder, the works of the Most High
	G "the sun, when appearing, announces, as it goes out	a marvelous instrument, the work of the Most High."
43:1	S "he made the sun to see and to praise	an instrument of wonder, a work of the Most High"
43:3	B "when it reaches noon, it causes to boil the world	and before its heat, who can withstand?"
	M "when it reaches noon, it causes to boil the world	and before its heat, who can withstand?"
43:3	G "at its midday it dries up the region	and before its burning heat who will stand?"

43:4a–43:4b
(43:3–43:4a) Syriac

43:3   S "at its mid of day it burns the land"   and before its heat, who is able to stand?"

43:4a   B "a furnace blasting *mhm mswq*"   the sun standing-forth sets-ablaze mountains."
Bm מצוק
שלה   סיר

43:4a   M "a furnace blasting casted works"   the ray of the sun ..."

43:4a   G "a furnace blasting in works of heat"   the sun three-times-as-much burns mountains."

43:4a   S "more than the furnace that blasts in the work of the blacksmith"   three-times more than that the sun burns mountains."
SL "as" *'yk*

43:4b   B "A tongue-of light brings to an end the inhabited-land"   by its light the eye is scorched."
Bm שוני
M "A tongue-of light brings-to-an-end the inhabited-land"   ..."

43:4b   G "Fiery vapors it blows out"   and (by) shining beams it dims the eyes."

43:5–43:6
(43:4b–43:6) Syriac

43:4b	S " its heat is like the vapor that pours down sL *nwr'*	and shines its rays and dazzles the eyes."
43:5	B "for great is YYY who made him(=the sun) Bm כי גדול עליון ועשׁהו	and his words direct his soaring." אבריו וכבדה
	M "for great is the Lord who made him	and his words
43:5	G "great is the Lord who made it	and by his word it hastens on (its) course."
43:5	S "great is the Lord who made it	and by the words of the Holy One it hastens on its course."
43:6	B "and also the moon moon seasons שׁבות Bm	a rule of limited-period and a sign forever." time to time
	M "and also the moon puts-on-course seasons-times	m.. ..."
43:6	G "and the moon he placed for its season	a marker of times and a sign of eternity."
43:6	S "the moon stands for seasons	a marker of times and an eternal sign."

43:7–43:8b
(43:7–43:8) Syriac

43:7	B "by them the appointed-season and times-of prescribed-days מועד במנינם	a delightful season in its turn-of the year.
	Bm בם	
	M "to him is the appointed-season and from him festival	
		…
43:7	G "From the moon is the sign-of the feast	a light that wanes upon reaching-the full."
43:7	S "For from the moon are the signs of festivals	a light that wanes at last."
43:8	B "month after its month it renews-itself	how fearful (it is) in its changing,"
	Bm וחדש כמו	מבחריו
	M "new-moon like its name re(news-itself)	
		…
43:8a	G "The month according to its name is	increasing marvelously in changes"
43:8	S "the month according to its name is	and it increases brilliantly in changes."
43:8b	B "A vessel of the host-of the clouds-of high	paving the firmament with its shining."
	Bm	מרצף

43:8b–43:10
(43:9–43:10) Syriac

43:8b	M "A vessel of the host-of the clouds-of high	paving ..."
43:9	G "A vessel putting-in-line in high	in the firmament of heaven shining forth."
43:9	S "An instrument of the host of high	that shines in the firmament of heaven."
43:9	B "The beauty-of heaven and the glory of a star Bm	and its light shines in the heights-of God." מאיר קין ואור
43:9	M "The beauty-of heaven is the glory of the stars	bearing testimony and turning-red in the hei(ghts).."
43:9	G "the beauty-of heaven is the glory of the stars	a world shining in the heights of the Lord."
43:10	S "An ornament of heaven and the praise of stars."	
43:10	B "by the word-of God it stands (in its) place Bm	and it does not run down in their morning watch ישמר"

43:10–43:12
(43:11

43:10 M "by the word-of the Lord it stands (in its) place   and it does not run down in their morning watch."
       G "by the words of the Holy One they will stand
         according to judgment   and they never are removed in their watches."

43:11 S "by the words of the Holy One they stand
         according to their judgment   and in their course, they do not dissemble."

43:11 B "Behold the rainbow and bless its maker   for very mighty (is it) in glory."
       Bm   עשוהו   נהדרה
       M "Behold the rainbow and bless its maker   for very majesti(c)..."
       G "behold the rainbow and bless he who made it   exceedingly beautiful in its brightness."

43:12 B הקה it encompasses with its glory   and the hand of God spreads out in ..."
       Bm הוד it encompasses with his glory
       M "the heavenly vault... with its glory   and the hand of God spreads out in might."

43:12–43:15

43:12	G "it encircles heaven with a glorious arc	the hands of the Most High stretches it out."
43:13	B "his might marks out lightning Bm "his might marks our the morning Bmm	and makes brilliant/directs the lightning-flashes-of..." וּמַבְרִיק יֹרֶה כְּבֹד
	M "his rebuke ..h the hail	נִצָּה אוֹרֵי and makes brilliant/directs the lightning-flashes of judgment."
43:13	G "by his command he sends forth snow	and speeds the lightnings of his judgment."
43:14	B "because he created a treasure-house Bm לְמַעֲנֵהוּ	and he-makes-fly..."
43:14	M "on his account he let loose a treasure house	and he-makes-fly clouds like bird-of-prey,"
	G "because of this storehouses are opened	and clouds he scares out like winged-birds."
43:15	B ... ..n ..l..	... עָ֫

43:15–43:17b

43:15
M "his might makes strong the cloud — and breaks up the stones-of-hail."
G "by his greatness he strengthens clouds — and breaks up the stones of hail."

43:16
B [" and by his strength he scolds mts. — his fear makes-sharp the south-wind."]
M and by his strength he shakes mts. — his word makes-sharp the south-wind."
43:16
G "and by his vision/appearances mts. are shaken — at his will south-wind will blow."

43:17a
B "the sound of his thunder makes weak his earth — winds-of the north, hurricane and tempest."
Bm "the sound of his thunder makes anguish his earth — עַל עֹל   מספח   וּסְעָרָה
M "the sound of his thunder makes anguish his earth — whirlwind, hurricane and tempest."
43:17a
G "the sound of his thunder put the earth in pain — also the tempest of the North wind and wind-storm."

43:17b
B .. birds flutters his snow — and like a locust-swarm settling יִשְׁכּוֹן

43:17b–43:19

Bm כארבה

M "like birds he lets fly his snow

and like a locust-swarm settling (is) its going down."

43:17b G "like birds settling down he sprinkles snow

and as a locust settles is its descending."

43:18 B "the beauty of its whiteness heals the eyes

its raining the heart is restless."

Bm יהגה

M "the beauty of its whiteness dazzles the eyes

and at its raining the heart is astonished."

43:18 G "(at) the beauty of its whiteness the eye marvels

and at its raining the heart will be in ecstasy."

43:19 B "and also hoar-frost like salt he lays down

and makes blossom like lapis-lazuli blossoms."

Bm יצעם

M " ... .. like salt he pours out

and makes sprout like a thorn blossoms."

43:20a–43:21

43:20a	G "and hoar-frost like salt upon the earth he pours	and freezing it becomes (like) the point of thorns."
	B "the coolness of the north wind he brings back	and like a skin-bag he condenses/curdles its source." מקוה
	Bm	
	M … .n he brings back	and like a clod he condenses/curdles the source,"
43:20a	G "The cold north wind will blow	and crystals will freeze over the water."
43:20b	B "upon every pool of water he overlays it	and like mail/armour the reservoir puts (it) on."
	M … pool of water he overlays it	…
43:20b	G "upon every pool of water he will deposit (it)	and as a breastplate the water will put it on."
43:21	B "the produce of the [mts.] like desolation he will burn	and pasture (its) sprouts like flame."
	Bm	ציר
	M … .m desolation yṣ..	…

43:21–43:24

43:21	G "he will devour mts. and desert he will burn	and will extinguish tender-grass like fire."
	M ? [ ] מ [שׁ]עֶ[ף] [ ]	
43:22	B healing all (is the) moistening of the cloud of dew	hastening to refresh (after) heat."
	Bm	טל פרויח כמ
43:22	G "a healing of all the mist hastens	the dew when it appears from the heat refreshes."
43:23	B "his thoughts ..šyq the-great-deep	and he stretched-out in the deep islands."
	Bm "his מהבאו	treasure
	M ... ? [ ] ח מתבאים [ ] אבר	
43:23	G "by his counsel he stilled the Abyss	and planted in it islands."
43:24	B "those who go down to the sea tell its extent	when our ears hear we are astonished."
	M ...	when our ears hear we are astonished."

43:24–43:27

43:24	G "Those who sail the sea describe its danger	and by the hearing of our ears we marvel."
43:25	B "There are marvels, the (most) amazing of his works	kinds of all living things and mighty things of the deep
	Bm מעשיו	
	M	... mighty things of Rahob
	G "there are incredible-things and marvelous works	kinds of all life, creatures of the deeps."
43:26	B "for his sake/because of him the messenger prospers	and by his word he works (his) will."
	Bm למענהו/למענו	
43:26	G "because of him his messenger prospers on-the-way	by his word all things are composed/hold together."
43:27	B "Yet all these and we have not finished	and the end of the matter(is) — He is everything."
	G "(though) we will speak much we will in no way arrive/reach end	the end of all the words — He is everything."

43:28-43:30b

43:28	B "it is revealed/evident still that not will we explore/it is explored Bm נהלה	for he is greater than all his works."
43:28	G "(for) glorifying, where will we be strong	for he is greater than all his works."
43:29	B "nw.. .. very very much Bm	and the miracles of his words." נפראיו
43:29	G "fearful is the Lord and very great	and marvelous (is) his power."
32:30a	B m.l. ... lift up (your) voice	in all you can for there is more."
43:30a	G "(when) praising the Lord exalt as much as you can for he will go beyond even still."	
43:30b	B "praising-ones renew (your) strength Bm מתחזקיו " " "	[and do not become weary for you will not explore, and do not become weary for you will not explore,"
43:30b	G "and exalting him, increase in strength	do not grow weary, for in no way can you do enough."

43:32–44:1

43:32	B (there are) "many more marvelous and powerful (things) than these	a few I have seen of his works."
43:32	G "many things hidden are greater than these	for fews things have we seen of his works."
43:31	G "who has seen him and will declare/describe him?	and who will magnify him as he is?
43:33	B "all things...	...l. ..."
43:33	G "for all things the Lord has made	and to the godly he gave wisdom."
44:1a	B "The praise of the Fathers of Old" G "A Hymn of the Fathers"	
44:1b	B "let me praise now men of piety	our fathers in their generations."
44:1	M ...	our fathers ...
44:1	G "let us praise now notable/honored men	and our fathers in the(ir) generation."

44:1-44:3b

44:1	S "and now I will praise men of renown	and our fathers that were in their generations."
44:2	B "great honor the most high allotted Bm לחם	and his greatness from days of old."
	M "great honor the Most High allotted	
44:2	G "great glory the Lord made	and his greatness from .. ..."
44:2	S "great honor he distributed to them	his greatness from the beginning." and all their greatness upon generations of old."
44:3a	B "generations of the earth in their reign Bm ורדי	and men of name in their might במלכם
44:3a	G "ruling in their kingdoms S	and men famous in power,"
44:3b	B "the counsellors in their discernment Bm ובעצת	and seers-of all in their prophecy."
	M "and they counsel in their discernment	and seers-of all in their proph(ecy)."

44:3b–44:5
(44:4–

44:3b	G "counseling in their understanding	and announcing in prophecies."
44:3	S "and they showed by their prophecy, signs and	counsels by their understanding."
44:4a	B "princes of nations in their discretion	and leaders in their distant lands."
	M "princes of a nation in their discretion	ורזני in their decrees."
44:4ab	G "rulers of people in counsels	and understanding of learning of the people."
44:4	S "wise-ones teaching in their wisdom	and rulers showing by their honor."
44:4b	B "wise-of conversation in their writing/instruction	speakers-of-proverbs in their service. במשרתה
	Bm במכתבים	
44:4c	M "wise of conversation in their writing	speakers-of-proverbs bm..
	G "wise words in their teaching	
44:5	B "inventors of psalm according to rule חק	those-who-set a proverb in a book."
	Bm	

44:5–44:7
(44:5–44:7) Syriac

44:5	M	"inventors of psalm according to .qw.	those who set a proverb in a book."
44:5	G	"seeking tunes of music	and presenting lyrics in writing;"
44:5	S	"regarding handlers of harps and lyres	and speakers of proverbs in the book of man(?)
44:6	B	"men of strength and supporters of power	living-at-ease upon their dwelling,"
44:6	M	"men of strength and supported by power	living-at ease ...
44:6	S	(?) of power and with sustenance of life	quiet upon their dwelling,"
44:6	G	"rich men furnished with strength	having peace in their dwellings."
44:7	B	"all these in their generation	and from their days (was) their recognition."
	Bm	were honored	and in their days
44:7	M	"all these in their generation were honored	...
44:7	G	"all these in (their) generations were honored	"and in their days their boasting."
44:7	S	"all these in their generations had honor	and in their days their glory."

44:8–44:9b

(44:8–44:9) Syriac

Verse	MS	Text	Syriac
44:8	B	"there are from them (some who) left a name	to recount (לספר) in their inheritance."
	Bm		לספרתה and לספורתה
	M	"there are from them (some who) left a name	lh.. ..."
44:8	G	"there are from them those who left a name	in order to declare praises."
44:8	S	"there are from them some who left a name	to declare (šʿ ʾ) upon their glory."
44:9a	B	"and there is from them he who does not have a memorial	and they came to an end when he ended."
	M	"and there is from them he who does not have a memorial	...
44:9a	G	"and there are (those) of whom there is not a memorial	and they perished as not beginning."
44:9	S	"and there are from them he who does not have a memorial	and he perished as those who perished."
	sL	plural	plural
44:9b	B	"as though they were not, they were	and their sons after them."
	M	"as though they were not, they were	...

44:9b–44:12
–44:11) Syriac

44:9b	G "and they became as not having become	and their children after them."
	S	
44:10	B "but, these (were) men of kindness/piety	and their hope shall not ..t"
44:10	M "but, these (were) men of kindness/piety	..."
44:10	G "but rather, these were men of pity/mercy	whose righteousnesses were not forgotten."
44:10	S "but, these (are/were) men of goodness and righteousness; their goodness will not fail.	
44:11	B "with their seed sure is their goodness	and their inheritance to.. ..."
44:11	M " if their seed sure is their goodness	wnh.. ..."
44:11	G "with their seed it will stand/remain	a good inheritance is their offspring."
44:11	S "and with their seed lasting/surviving their good	their root to the sons of their sons."
	B	
44:12	M "in their covenant stands their seed	and their descendants...

44:12–44:15
(44:12–44:14) Syriac

44:12	G	"in their covenants stands (?ἔστη) their seed	and their children, for their sake,"
44:12	S	"in their covenants stands their seed	and the sons of their sons in good works."
44:13	B	"forever their memorial will stand	and their righteousness will not..."
44:13	M	"forever their seed will stand	and their honor will not be blotted out."
44:13	G	"forever their seed will abide	and their glory will not be blotted out."
44:13	S	"and forever their memory (is) surviving	and their glory will not be forgotten."
44:14	B	"... .l.. ...	... l.. and generations."
44:14	M	"and their body in peace was gathered/buried	and their name is alive from generation to generation."
44:14	G	"and their bodies in peace were buried	and their name lives unto generations."
44:14	S	"their bodies in peace were gathered/buried	but their name (is) alive from generation to generation."
44:15	B	["their wisdom the assembly recounts	and their praises the congregation relates."]

44:15–44:17
(44:15–44:17, 18a) Syriac

44:15	M ... assembly	
44:15	G "their wisdom the peoples declare	and their praise the congregation relates."
44:15	S "their praise the people will declare."	and the(ir) praise the congregation will announce.
44:16	B "Enoch was found perfect	and he walked with YYY and was taken,
	G "Enoch was pleasing to the Lord and was transposed/moved	a sign of knowledge for all generations."
44:17a	B "Noah the righteous was found blameless	an example of repentance for generations."
	Bm	for a time of destruction he was the continuator."
		בעת
	M "Noah the righteous was found blameless	.b ...
44:17a	G "Noah was found perfect and righteous	in a time of wrath he became the exchange."
44:17, 18a	S "Noah the righteous was found in his generation perfect	in the time of the flood he was the substitute in the world."

44:17b B "for his sake there was a remnant and by his covenant the flood ceased."

  M "b. ... ...

44:17b G "because of this (man) there became a remnant for the earth when the cataclysm came."

44:18b, 19 S "and because of him there was deliverance and God swore that there would not again be a flood.

  sL îmā, "to him"

5
The Syriac Version and Its Relationship to the Other Texts and Versions

A. OMISSIONS, ADDITIONS AND ALTERATIONS IN THE SYRIAC VERSION

The Syriac Version as a whole omits about 200 lines which the Hebrew and Greek (Greek I) have in common, i.e., about 1/9 of the Hebrew/Greek is missing. However, at the same time, Syriac adds over forty lines not found in Greek or Hebrew! Often too, where there are no omissions, there are significant additions or alterations in the wording. This section (A) will be addressed to the question of omissions, additions, and alterations in the Syriac Version of the sections of Ben Sira under study, 39:27–44:17.

Passages Contrary to Belief in Life after Death

As a rule, passages which cast doubt on life after death are omitted in the Syriac Version. In some cases, the preceding and/or following lines are altered somewhat or additions are made to compensate for the material omitted.

41:4b. B/Bm/M/G all preserve the passage with fairly clear meaning: "whether a thousand years, a hundred, or ten, there are no reproaches/convictions in Sheol." Life is over at death, and there is no more punishment or reproach. ἐλεγμός/ἐλεγξις carries the idea of "conviction" for a crime[2] and תוכחה that of "punishment."[3] The Syriac completely drops the passage; in fact, the Beirut reprint for the Mosul Bible skips from verse 6 (=41:4a) to verse 8 (=41:5) with no verse numbered 7.

41:9a,9b. The Hebrew materials for 9a (B, Bm[1], Bm[2], M), though fragmentary, jointly state that "fruitfulness" is only for destruction and "offspring" only for a sigh or groan. The Greek confirms this, while in the second half of the line

---

[1] Smend: 1906, II, p. cxxxvii; Winter: 1977, p. 237.
[2] Liddell-Scott: 1968, pp. 530f.
[3] K-B: 1958, p. 1021; Jastrow: 1950, II, pp. 1652f.

it places the curse on the person born rather than his offspring. Again, in 9b, the Hebrew and Greek texts support one another: "if you die, it is only for a curse." Syriac found this a far too negative view of death and afterlife[4] — 9a and 9b are both omitted. To compensate, Syriac adds two lines, the first of which shows an awareness of the passage left out ("fruitfulness," "offspring"): "A fertile woman (is) for the joy of her people" and "but if a lawless father dies, his upright sons will not mourn over him." This addition in Syriac is a variant of vs. 7.[5]

41:10a. Syriac reduces "all that is nothing returns to nothing; thus the ungodly from nothing (returns to) nothing" (B, M) to "for the wicked, his end is destruction." Any notion of nothingness after death is repressed here. The influence of Greek "destruction" (ἀπώλειαν) can be seen in the Syriac ('bdn').[6]

41:11. The Hebrew "vain (is) man in his body" is dropped in Syriac and what remains, "but the name of those who do good will not ever be lost," forms a good second half to the Syriac of 41:10a. Again, the Syriac appears to be influenced by the Greek in the wording it preserves.[7]

41:12. To compensate for the previous omission, Syriac adds "because gifts and allies perish." Hebrew "thousands of stores of wisdom" becomes "thousands of stores of gold" in Greek, and the Syriac, following Greek somewhat, renders "thousand treasures of fraud (*'ēṭā*)."

41:13-19. Syriac omits this entire section. The passage argues that only a good name endures (41:13) and then it presents supporting material on shame or discretion designed to help one establish a good name. The Syriac drops even the supporting material and adds nothing in compensation. To the Syriac translator, this section was not only suspect for its negative implication regarding resurrection, but also very difficult to understand; hence, it was dropped.

44:9b. 44:9a in Hebrew refers to "those who have no memorial" and 9b continues, "they became as though they were not." Syriac keeps 9a, but eliminates 9b, which apparently was offensive to belief in life after death.

Passages Descriptive of Nature and Natural Phenomena

39:30c. There is a great deal of confusion and perhaps some rearrangement in these lines. The Syriac which is preserved at this point properly goes with the

---

[4] For the association of the realm of the dead with "sighing," see Penar: 1975, p. 70.

[5] Smend: 1906, II, p. 384.

[6] This is the only instance in which ἀπώλειαν in Greek corresponds to *'bdn'* in Syriac, but it is clear that Syriac dearts from Hebrew in the same way as does the Greek. Smend: 1907[1], pp. 28–29; Winter: 1976, pp. 4–5.

[7] Greek ἐξαλείψειν matches Syriac *t' '* in four (23:26; 39:9, 41:11; 44:13) of eight times that the Greek word appears. Smend: 1907[1], pp. 89–90.

next verse in Hebrew. This means the Syriac simply drops out the words, "all these for their use were created, and they are in supply for the time they will be summoned."[8] In the light of the fact that the entire unit in praise of creation (39:12-35) is preserved in Syriac, 39:30c was probably dropped for the simple mechanical reason that it is so similar to what follows in the next line.

42:15–44:1a. The entire forty-third chapter is encompassed by a section on God's work in nature. This section begins at 42:15 and continues through 44:1a. There are various changes and omissions in the Syriac:

42:18 In a passage referring to God's knowledge of all things, Syriac is careful not to follow Greek, which implies that God must look into a "sign" of the future.

B a   the deep and the heart he searches out,
   b   and into all their secrets he examines.

M a   the deep and the heart he searches out,
   b   and into their secrets he examines;
   c   for knowledge is to Elyon all
      (Yadin: for Most High possesses knowledge)
   d   and seeing what *comes* ('th) upon *eternity.*

S a   the deep and the heart he explores,
   b   and all the hidden things of man,
      as the sun, are revealed before him,
   c   because nothing is hidden from God;
   d   and there appear before him all that *comes* to the *world.*

G a   the abyss and heart he traced out,
   b   and into their crafty plans he considered;
   c   for Most High knew all to know
   d   and looked into the sign of eternity.

The Syriac obviously disagrees with the Greek understanding of *'tywt* as coming from *'wt* ("sign") and understands it as *'t* ("to come"): everything is revealed before God, including what is yet to happen.[9]

42:21b, 22, 23 Syriac omits "nothing added and nothing taken away; he does not need any counsel" (42:21b) and "are not all his works lovely, even to a

---

[8] Indeed, so does *The New American Bible* (1976).

[9] I was alerted to this difference by M. Winter (1977, I, p. 249); however, I disagree with his remark that Syriac *changes* anything. In fact, it *preserves* the original in spite of a usual dependence on Greek in this section.

spark or glimpse of appearance?" (42:22) However, considerable expansion can be seen in 42:23, which bears a relationship to the words lost in 42:21b and 22.

43:2 Syriac (*mrym'*), Greek (ὕψιστος), and Masada (עליון) agree ("Most High") against B (yyy)![10] Both times that *mrym'* appears in Syriac (also 7:9b), it corresponds to ὕψιστος. Thus, it is possible to see Greek influence on Syriac here. In fact, all of 43:1-10 is very close to the Greek.

43:9 Syriac omits (with reference to the stars), "its light shines in the heights of God," the second half of the line.

43:11-44:1a This entire unit, slightly more than half the material on God's work in creation (42:15-44:1a), is dropped from the Syriac text, though the whole of the creation material is well-preserved in Hebrew and Greek.

The omissions, additions, and alterations in passages descriptive of nature and natural phenomena provide this information regarding the Syriac Version:

1) There are times when the version is expansionist and periphrastic;
2) passages difficult to understand are often simply dropped;
3) a particularly long passage which is somewhat redundant will be greatly reduced; and,
4) in difficult passages, the Greek is consulted, but not to the extent of introducing an error.

Passages Implying that Wisdom was Created

The Arian slogan, "there was a time when he was not" (ἦν ποτε ὅτε οὐκ ἦν), was well-known to the Syrian Christians of the fourth century and after![11] Arius had argued that the Godhead is one and its essence (οὐσία) cannot be shared. Hence, Christ (Word and Wisdom) is a creation of God and not self-existent. He came into being before time and the rest of creation, but He nevertheless had a beginning.

This position was condemned at Nicea (325 A.D.), but led to some further controversies in the eastern church. There are some passages in the Syriac of Ben Sira which seem to indicate a Christian hand at work attempting to avoid

---

[10] ὕψιστος represents אל eight times, YYY four times, עליון twice, and המלך once. It corresponds to Syriac *'lh'* nine times, *mr'* once, *mrym'* twice, *mry'* once, *'ly'* twice, and *šmy'* once. Smend: 1907[1], p. 236; Winter: 1976, pp. 573-574. Yadin believes Ms. B to be corrupt, the true text being preserved in M, G, and S. Yadin: 1965, p. 29 (English).

[11] Kelley: 1960, pp. 226-231; Stevenson: 1965, pp. 340-354; see M. Simonetti, *Studi sull' Arianismo* (Rome, 1965), pp. 9-87 (cited by Winter: 1977, II, p. 505 n. 9).

any statements that could appear to endorse the Arian heresy or any heresies similar to it.

39:32. This verse falls in a context of praise to God for the goodness and usefulness of all his creation and his actions (39:12-35). It is possible, too, that Wisdom is speaking in the first person in this long passage, and thus the things said about Wisdom are very important in the light of the controversies.[12]

B (Hist.   a Therefore from the beginning I stood assured (*htysbty*),
Dict.)[13]   b and I considered it and in writing I set it down.

B (Lévi)[14] a Therefore from the beginning I was held back (*ht'kbty*),
          b and I considered it and in writing I set it down.
M   a...
       b...........................I...........................

G   a Because from the beginning I was fixed/set (ἐστηρίχθην)
       b and I thought it over and in writing I left it.

S   a Because from the beginning they were created (*'tbryw*).
       b Understand, O men, that in a book all these are written.

All these witnesses, except Syriac, have the verbs in first singular. Whether they intended to imply that Wisdom was "created" "from the beginning" is hard to say. In fact, it is not even clear which verb was used at the end of the first line: Lévi reads *ht'kbty* and Smend and the *Historical Dictionary of the Hebrew Language* read *htysbty*. *'kb* is quite rare; *ysb* more common.[15] This is the only place in Ben Sira where στηρίζειν would represent either of these words.[16]

Br' is very common in the Syriac of Ben Sira, but never is it representing either *'kb* or *ysb*, unless here.[17] In 25% of the cases it represents Hebrew *br'*, and in 39:28 above, *br'* is used in Syriac to mean "create." Consequently, regardless of which word was used in the original Hebrew, the Syriac writer took either or both the Hebrew and Greek to mean creation. In order to avoid any implied heresy regarding the creation of Wisdom, he changed the verb to a passive plural,

---

[12] Winter: 1977, II, p. 502.
[13] Historical Dictionary: 1973; Smend: 1906, I, p. 38.
[14] Lévi 1898, 1904.
[15] Jastrow: 1950, I & II; K-B: 1958.
[16] Smend: 1907[1], p. 216.
[17] Of thirty instances, Syriac *br'* represents Hebrew *br'* seven times, *nsr* seven times, *'sh* five times, *hlq* three times, *ns'* once, and once each *yld*, *ys'*, *yb'*, *gdl*, *'l*, *swr*, *pqd*. Winter: 1976, pp. 102-104.

referring to all the works of God mentioned earlier[18] — *they* are created, not Wisdom.

42:21-23. Again, in the section on God's work in creation (42:15–44:1a), there appears to be cause for concern by the Syrian writer regarding the Arian heresy. The lines in question here are 21a and 23:

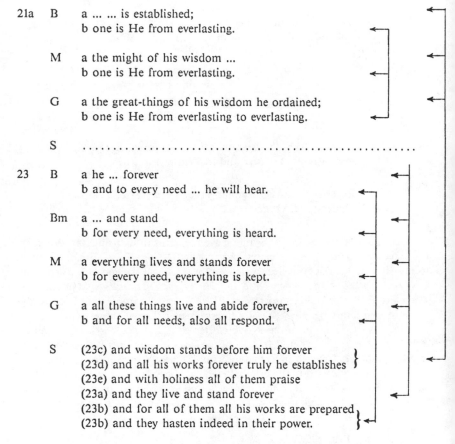

21a   B   a ... ... is established;
           b one is He from everlasting.

      M   a the might of his wisdom ...
           b one is He from everlasting.

      G   a the great-things of his wisdom he ordained;
           b one is He from everlasting to everlasting.

      S   ....

23   B   a he ... forever
           b and to every need ... he will hear.

      Bm   a ... and stand
           b for every need, everything is heard.

      M   a everything lives and stands forever
           b for every need, everything is kept.

      G   a all these things live and abide forever,
           b and for all needs, also all respond.

      S   (23c) and wisdom stands before him forever
           (23d) and all his works forever truly he establishes
           (23e) and with holiness all of them praise
           (23a) and they live and stand forever
           (23b) and for all of them all his works are prepared
           (23b) and they hasten indeed in their power.

It can be seen from the above correspondences that Syriac 23a and 23b relate to Hebrew and Greek 23a and 23b, but that Syriac 23c and 23d go back

---

[18] Smend simply calls it a bad translation on the part of the Syriac writer. Smend: 1906, II, p. 366. Peters, likewise, feels it is a mistranslation based on 39:25 (*ḥlq mrʾš*). Peters: 1902, p. 171.

to Hebrew and Greek 21a. It is in these latter passages that significant alterations take place.

Syriac is careful to avoid any implication that Wisdom was created; instead, "Wisdom stands before him forever," and it is "all his works" which are "established," not Wisdom! This appears to be an intentional change motivated by a theological concern.

Passages Regarding Women

42:14. The section 42:9-14 is a warning to a father on how to care for his daughter. The view of women as a whole expressed here is very low—they are not to be trusted and they tend to lead one another astray. Vs. 14 is completely omitted in Syriac:

B   a   Better is the badness of a man than the goodness of a woman
     b   and a daughter who fears (B: *hrp*, Bm¹: *hrp*, Bm²: *hpr*)[19] from
       all (*tby'*)[20] disgrace (*'šh*).[21]

M   a   Better is the badness of a man than the goodness of a woman
     b   and a daughter who fears (*phd*) from all disgrace (*hrp*).

G   a   Better (is) the evil of man than the woman who does good,
     b   and a woman who brings shame and disgrace.

Apparently the Syriac writer found this criticism of women too harsh and so he eliminated it. The Syriac omits, also, 36:21-26 which, though it contains high praise for a good wife, it begins with a rather derogatory remark about women as compared to men: "any man may be chosen as a husband, but there is always a prettier girl" (36:21/26). Our translator appears not to have been quite as chauvinistic as the original author.[22]

---

[19] Bm attempted to make sense of the corrupted B text. Yadin: 1965, p. 25. *hpr*[II], "be ashamed," K-B: 1958, p. 322; Jastrow: 1950, I, p. 493.

[20] Copyist corruption of *mkwl*. Yadin: 1965, p. 25. Baumgarten suggests for M "and a daughter is more worrisome than a son with regard to disgrace (*mbn lhrph*)," or "and a daughter, more than a son, bringeth disgrace (*wbt mhprt mbn lhrph*)." 1967-1968: pp. 326-327.

[21] Crept in from first line and crowded out *hrph*. Yadin: 1965, p. 25.

[22] Syriac preserves in full chapter 26 on the good and bad wife. However, that chapter does not contain such negative remarks on womankind in general.

42.10b. This passage, 42:10b, is missing in Syriac. The Hebrew is rather broken, but the Greek is complete in both 10a and 10b. Thus, the Syriac writer has chosen not to follow Greek, but simply to eliminate a passage not clear in the Hebrew. In fact, there is a rearrangement of some lines in Greek, but Syriac preserves the Hebrew order. 10a is slightly expanded in Syriac to compensate for the loss in 10b.

10a	B	In her young-womanhood lest she be fooled (*tpwth, pual*),[23] and in the house ..1.. 1.. ...
	Bm	be fooled (*ttpth, hith.*)
	Bm	In her young-womanhood lest she be fooled (*ttpth, hith.*)
	Bm	,..house of husband (*b'l*) 1.. be forgotten (*tnšh*).
	M	In her young-womanhood lest she be defiled (*thl*), and regarding her husband (*'yšh*)...she turn aside (*tšth*).
	G	In virginity, lest she be profaned, and in her father's house she become pregnant.
	S	In her young-womanhood lest she devise plans, and regarding her husband (*b'l*) lest she be unfaithful (*šth*) in her mind and go after another man.
10b	B	In the house of her father lest..., and in the house of her husband (*'yšh*)...she be barren (*t'sr*).
	Bm	father lest she be insolent (*phzh*)
	Bm	In the house of her father lest..., and in the house of her husband (*'yšh*) lest she be barren (*t'sr*).
	M	House of her father lest she bear-seed (*tzry'*), and in her husband (*b'l*) ...
	G	Being with her husband, lest she go astray; and being married, lest she be barren.
	S	(10a expanded; 10b missing.)

In the second half of 10a, one can see that M, G, and S are very close:

M	"and regarding her husband (*'yšh*),...she turn aside (*tšth*)"[24]
G	"being with her husband, lest she go astray (παραβαινειν)"[25]
S	"and regarding her husband (*b'l*) lest she be unfaithful (*tšt'*)"[26]

[23] Jastrow: 1950, II, pp. 1252–1253; K-B: 1958, p. 786.

[24] *šth/šty/sth* "to deviate, turn away from, be faithless" Jastrow: 1950, II, pp. 972, 1552–1553.
sth "to stray, turn aside" K-B: 1958, p. 918.
šth/šty "to go astray, be demented, foolish" Jastrow: 1950, II, pp. 1552–1553.

[25] παραβαινειν Here is the only place it represents *sth/šth*. Smend: 19071, pp. 178–179.

[26] J. Payne Smith: 1903, p. 573.

Thus S has preserved the original form of 10a in both its arrangement and wording. S and all of the Hebrew materials agree in arrangement; M, G, and S in the wording.

42:12a. S makes a slight alteration, apparently for the sake of modesty: "figure" (*t'r*) becomes "heart" (1b).

B   "to every male, let her not give (her) figure."
M   "to every male, let her not reveal (her) figure."
G   "to every person do not look for beauty."
S   "to every man do not reveal what is in your heart."

Thus we see that the Syriac writer was modest in his comments about women and was also careful to avoid remarks that were too degrading to members of the female sex.[27]

Passages Referring to the Great Men

There are a number of omissions in the Syriac version of chapter 44, the praise of Israel's great men.

44:1a. B and G preserve a title for this section; M has lost some lines here, but it is impossible to determine whether the title was present.[28] S lacks the title.

B   "The praise of the Fathers of Old"
G   "A Hymn of the Fathers"

44:3a. M and S lack this line:[29]

B   "generations (*dwry*) of the earth in their reign, and men of
      name in their might."
Bm   "rulers of (*rwdy*)"
G   "ruling in their kingdoms, and men famous in their power."

---

[27] McKeating suggests that Ben Sira was representative of wisdom writers of his time and faithfully describes Jewish social and family life during the Greek period: A woman's role was domestic and a bad wife was anyone who could not fulfill the role well. 1973: pp. 191ff. The Syriac translator may well have endorsed that general view, but he certainly did not preserve the severely negative remarks about womankind.

[28] Yadin 1965, p. 34.

[29] Copyist of M probably omitted this by mistake since the next line in B and M start the same. Yadin: 1965, p. 35.

44:4a. This line, though preserved in B, M, and G, is missing in Syriac.

B   "princes of nations in their discretion, and leaders in their distant lands"[30]

M   "princes of a nation in their discretion, and leaders in their decrees."[31]

G   "rulers of people in counsels, and understanding of learning of the people."

44:9b. Here B, M and G all preserve the line, but Syriac omits it.

B   "as though they were not, they were, and their sons after them."

M   "as though they were not, they were, ..."

G   "and they became as not having become, and their children after them."

The reason for omitting this passage is probably due to its negative implication regarding the resurrection.[32]

44:15. Syriac drops only the first half of the line, which is redundant to one not so concerned with Hebrew parallelism.

Bm   "their wisdom the assembly recounts, and their praise the congregation relates."

M   "...   assembly, and their praise the congregation relates."

G   "their wisdom the peoples declare, and their praise the congregation will announce."

S   "their praise the peoples will declare"

44:16. Again both M and S are missing the passage, this time referring to Enoch:[33]

---

[30] *mrhqwtm > mhqqtm,* see n. 31.

[31] Perhaps originally *mhqqtm,* "decrees." Yadin: 1965, p. 35.

[32] Smend: 1906, II, p. 420. Peters feels it was simply shortened by Syriac to avoid redundance. Peters: 1902, p. 228.

[33] Bickell feels the verse should be deleted since it is strophically isolated; Smend responds that it belongs since it shows the beginning of a new era; Syriac's omission is not telling since it omits several passages in the section. Smend: 1906, II, pp. 421–22. However, neither of these scholars would have known that 44:16 was missing from Ms. M.

B   "Enoch was found perfect, and he walked with YYY and was
     taken;
                         a sign of knowledge for all generations"
G   "Enoch was pleasing to the Lord and was transposed;
                         an example of repentance for generations."

Later, at 49:14, B (*hnyk!*) and S (*hnwk*) refer to Enoch, though S drops 14b.

The passages omitted in this section admit to at least three possible explanations:

1.   S occasionally shows that its Hebrew *Vorlage* was akin to M;
2.   S omits some lines simply because of the abundance of such
      phrases in the section and to avoid redundancy; and,
3.   Perhaps there is a bias against the Jewish people and their
      law.[34]

Passages Regarding Poverty and Wealth[35]

40:8, 9, 10. Verse eight is hardly readable in Hebrew, but it is well-preserved in Greek. Verse nine, preserved in B and G, though now lost in M, is dropped in Syriac.

8   G   "with all flesh from man to beast,
          and upon sinners seven times (more) than these:"
9   B   "pestilence and bloodshed, fever and sword,
          devastation and destruction, evil and death."
10   B   "for the wicked was created evil,
          and on his account annihilation (Smend: does not)[36] depart."

---

[34] Winter: 1977, II, pp. 494–498.

[35] See Winter: 1977, I, pp. 244–249. Winter adds 44:6 to this list, rendering Hebrew and Syriac as follows:

B and M   "men of wealth (*'nšy hyl*) and secure in strength, living at ease in their
                 dwelling places."
S   "in gatherings of strength and at peace in their work."

He then suggests that Syriac dropped *hyl* because of his bias toward wealth. However, it seems to me that Syriac does preserve here exactly what we have in Hebrew if one includes the last two words inadvertently attached to vs. 5 in Syriac:

S   "men of power (*tuqpa*) and with the sustenance of life/wealth (*hayla*),
                 living quietly upon their dwelling."

Thus, we do not have in this verse evidence of the Syriac writer's aversion to wealth.

[36] Smend: 1906, II, p. 372.

Syriac drops vv. 9 and 10[37] and alters vs. 8 to read:

> "with all the sons of flesh their anxiety is with them; *riches* disturb their sleep."

40:28. The Hebrew of this verse clearly denigrates begging:

> B/Bm "my son, the life of a beggar do not live,
> better is one dead than rejected."

But the Syriac turns the coin to the other side and advises not to turn a beggar away:

> S   "my son, whoever begs from you do not refuse him; you will
>   not do good to kill, rather it is good only to cause life."

It is quite clear from these two passages that the Syriac translator was suspicious of wealth and not averse to poverty. Perhaps, in dropping 40:10, he was afraid to identify the "poor" with the "wicked," since, in his view, poverty was an accepted, if not recommended, state of being.

Other Passages

Several other passages not classified in the categories above will be mentioned here for the sake of completeness.

40:6a, b.

6a   B   "a little idle time, for a moment he may rest;
          and from an interval in dreams ..š (Smend: *ngrš*, "is
          disturbed.")
     G   "a little, like none, in rest;
          and from that/after that in sleep(s) as in a restless day."
6b   B   "a little deceived by the vision of his soul;
          like a refugee in.. ... the pursuer."
     G   "disturbed by a vision of his heart/mind
          as one having escaped from battle front.
     S   "he deliberates in a vision of the night,
          like a man who escapes from before the pursuer."

---

[37] Peters feels vv. 9 and 10 have fallen out of Syriac accidentally (1902: p. 177). Smend believed v. 8 in Syriac to be a variant to 7b, which then caused vv. 9 and 10 to be dropped (1906, II, p. 371). However, the M manuscript shows that verses 7, 8, 9, and 10 all existed at that time, and these are confirmed by Greek. It appears that the alterations and omissions in Syriac were intentional.

The Syriac writer has eliminated 6a since it is so similar to 5b, but preserves 6b, even though in Hebrew 6a and 6b are tied together with *m 't*. For the sake of economy, this stylistic feature has been overlooked in Syriac.[38]

40:26b-27. Between strong exhortations to fear God (40:26ab and 40:27), the Syriac writer felt compelled to insert an even stronger exhortation. This insertion is not supported by B, M, or G.

> "The fear of God over everything is exalted; seize it, my son,
> and do not slacken because there is nothing like it."

41:13-28. It was mentioned above that vs. 13 was dropped in Syriac due to its implication regarding resurrection. Here it should be noted that the rest of the passage, 14-28, is likewise missing in Syriac. This section deals with proper shame—when and when not to be ashamed. Syriac adds at 41:19c and 20 several lines which are reminiscent of the Greek and Hebrew of these verses; this shows that the translator was aware of the longer passage, but chose for reasons of economy not to preserve it.

> 41:19c, 20 Syriac:
> "all who inquire regarding his welfare and he remains silent,
> that one is a great robber."
>
> "a greeting that you give him,
> he will not answer you;
> a deposit that you give him,
> how will he return (it) to you?"

B. TEXTUAL AFFINITIES

Yadin has catalogued in three detailed tables the relationships between M, B text, and Bm.[39] A summary of his results is as follows:

Table 1: M and Bm agree in wording 48 times against B text.

M and Bm agree in wording 4 times when B text is missing.

Table 2: M and B text agree in wording 39 times against Bm.

Table 3: In 90 cases, M diverges from both B text and Bm.

---

[38] Smend feels the Syriac writer has misunderstood Hebrew *m 't 't* for *y 't* (= *y 's*) and has thus used *mtmlk* ("deliberate") 1906, II, p. 370. Perhaps we have a rather free rendering of a Hebrew doublet (6a, 6b), blended into one in Syriac (6b).

[39] Yadin: 1965, pp. 7-9, 11-13.

He concludes from this study that B text and Bm, largely on the basis of their agreement with M, both represent the original Hebrew version.[40] Masada and B text are to be preferred over Bm.[41]

Here we will present material on the relationships of S to M, G, and B. In the closing chapter, Chapter 6: Concluding Statements, we will draw conclusions on the Syriac Version and its relationship to the Greek and Hebrew materials.

Cases in which S (in omissions, additions, alterations)
Follows G or M or Both

S	G	M	Comment:
39:28b	39:28b	39:28b	Missing in B
40:1a (created)	40:1a (created)	LOST[42]	G and S same verb
40:1b (their)	40:1b (their)	LOST	G and S same person
40:2	40:2	LOST	Missing in B
40:4 (crown)	40:4 (crown)	LOST	B—turban and ornament
40:14	40:14		{ S close to G; B and M considerably different
40:16		40:16	"herb" (S) = "green grass" (M) against "rain" (B)
40:26b	40:26b		{ βοήθειαν = *m'drn*[43]
41:4a (*ḥarta*)		41:4a (*qs*)	"end" (S and M); *ḥlq* in B
41:10 (destruction)	41:10 (destruction)		ἀπωλειαν = *'abdānā*
41:11b (bad name)	41:11b (bad name)		Hebrew refers to "kind name"; Greek and Syriac to "bad name"
41:12	41:12		Hebrew refers to "wisdom"; Greek to "gold" and Syriac to "gifts"

[40] Yadin: 1965, p. 7.

[41] Yadin: 1965, p. 9.

[42] I.e., according to Yadin, this verse existed in Ms. M but has been LOST due to deterioration.

[43] Syriac follows Greek here, as in 40:24. Smend: 1906, II, p. 379. *m'drn'* appears three times in the Syriac of Ben Sira (12:17b; 40:24, 26); each time it corresponds to βοήθεια/βοηθεῖν. Winter: 1976, p. 466; Smend: 1907¹, p. 37.

S	G	M	Comment
42:10a	42:10a	42:10a	G, S, M—"turn aside, go astray"
42:12	42:12		B and M refer to female "figure"; S, to "heart" and G, to "beauty" in general
42:17a		42:17a	"his miracles" (S and M) against "the miracles" (B)
42:18b	42:18b	42:18b	Missing in B
43:2 (*mrym'*)	43:2ff (ὑφιστος)	43:2 (*'lywn*)	B has YYY
43:4a	43:4a		G and S "three times more"
43:4b	43:4b		G and S "vapor" G and S active voice: "Shining its rays, it dims/dazzles the eyes."
43:5 (*mry'*)	43:5 (κυριος)	43:5 (*'dny*)	B has YYY; Bm, *'lywn*[44]
43:6	43:6		In B and M, moon is subject and seasons is object; in G and S, seasons is indirect object; in G, moon is object; in S, it is subject of intransitive verb
43:7	43:7		G and S almost identical in wording
43:8a (name)	43:8a (name)	43:8a (name)	S, G, M "like its name" S, G "it is" B, M "renews itself"
43:8b	43:8b		S and G do not mention "clouds"
43:10 (*Qdyš'*)	43:10 (ἁγιος)		S and G "Holy One"
44:1a (missing)		44:1a (missing)	This line, present only in B and G, is the introductory title to the praise of the fathers.

[44] Κυριος corresponds to Syriac *mry'* 52 times, to *'lh'* 83 times, *bry'* twice, *šmy'* once, *'wtr'* once, *'ly* once. Smend: 1907¹, pp. 141–44.
mry' represents YYY/YY 24 times; *'lhym* seven times; *'l* four times; *'dwn* Bm once, M twice, B once; *'l 'lywn/'lywn* three times. Winter: 1976, pp. 381–85.
Not much can be proved by this information regarding the relationship of S to Hebrew, but it does show the closeness of S and G.

S	G	M	Comment
44:12	44:12	44:12	Missing in B
44:13		44:13	Glory (*'iqar'*)[45] and honor
			(*kbwd*) in S and M;
			righteousness (*sdqh*) in B

The results can be summarized as follows:
1. S and G agree against M twelve times;
2. S, G, and M agree against B seven times;
3. S and M agree against B and G one time;
4. S and M agree against B four times; and,
5. S and G agree against B four times when M is lost.

Cases in which S and M Correspond
Regardless of Variances in B, Bm and G

In the following passages, which are always present in B and G, S follows M consistently in the presence or absence of the verses:

Verses present in S and M: 44:1b, 2, 3b, 4b, 5, 6, 7, 8, 9a, 10, 11, 13, 14, 17a, 17b
Verses absent in S and M: 44:3a, 16

In 44:12, M, G, and S follow each other, even though there is no B or Bm for this verse.
In 44:15, M, G, S, and Bm (no B) are present.
Thus, from 44:1a–17b, S and M correspond to each other in presence or absence of lines regardless of the variances in B, Bm, and G. The only exception is 44:4a and 4b where S condenses the two into one.

The Relationship Between S and B

In practically all the instances where B and M agree, S also agrees. The following is a list of such instances. This list includes cases where M is not lost, but excludes all cases where any text is too corrupt to make a clear decision. As would be expected, S makes some slight changes; its renderings rarely correspond exactly to the Hebrew.

S = B = M
39:29, 30
40:15
41:1a, 1b, 2a, 3

---

[45] *'iqar'* never represents *sdqh* in the Syriac of Ben Sira, unless of course this is an example. Rather, *'iqar'* represents *kbwd* in practically all the instances. Winter: 1976, pp. 298–99.

42:13, 15a, 16, 17b, 18, 19, 20, 24, 25
43:3
44:1b, 2 (S = Bm), 4bα, 6, 7, 8, 9a, 10, 11, 17a

S = B
40:20 This passage is LOST from M, but S and B agree against G.

The results of section B may be summarized as follows:
S = G ≠ M, twelve times
S = G = M ≠ B, seven times
S = M ≠ B and G, one time
S = M ≠ B, four times
S = G ≠ B (no M), four times
S = M while B, Bm, G vary (44:1a–17b, except 44.4ab)
S = B = M, 27 times
S = B (M LOST), one time

6
Concluding Statements

A. THE TEXTS AND VERSIONS

What is the place of the Syriac Version of Ben Sira in the history of the transmission of that book from its original Hebrew text down to its extant forms in Hebrew, Greek, and Syriac? This is a difficult and complex question; however, some answers can be given as a result of this study. These answers are summarized below.

The Syriac Version of Ben Sira was translated from a Hebrew original which had affinities to both M and B.[1] It was not translated from Greek, but certainly it was influenced by the Greek Version.[2] In fact, not only was the author guided by the Greek Version known as GI, but there is evidence he was aware of readings from GII.[3]

At an early date, before the appearance of GII and Syriac, two forms of the Hebrew text developed (HI and HII). The Syriac Version shows a relationship to each.[4]

A diagram will illustrate these above-mentioned relationships:

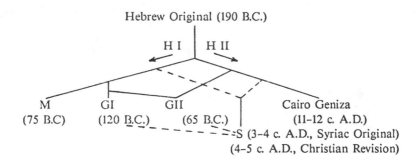

Hebrew Original (190 B.C.)

H I | H II

| M | GI | GII | Cairo Geniza |
| (75 B.C) | (120 B.C.) | (65 B.C.) | (11–12 c. A.D.) |

S (3–4 c. A.D., Syriac Original)
(4–5 c. A.D., Christian Revision)

[1] See Chapters 1, D. and 5, B.
[2] See Chapter 5, B.
[3] See Chapter 1, D.
[4] See Chapters 1, E., Recent Study; and 5, B.

Thus, we can conclude that the Syriac Version was based on a form of the Hebrew text earlier than that of the Cairo manuscripts on the basis of its many affinities with ms. M. However, we can also say that the Hebrew text used by the Syriac translator was not as early as ms. M due to its affinities with B and Bm and its apparent awareness of both GI and GII readings.

B. THE ORIGIN AND REVISION OF THE SYRIAC VERSION

It is also true, however, that the Syriac Version shows considerable independence of any of the other versions or manuscripts. Apart from many incidental changes, there are at least 29 instances in which the Syriac writer has gone his own way intentionally.[5] These changes give some indication of the origin and transmission of the Syriac Version.[6]

The first Syriac Version of Ben Sira was probably produced by Jewish scholars for Syriac-speaking Jews. Perhaps this was done in the region of Edessa where there had been a Jewish community since A.D. 40.[7] Syriac versions of the Bible were known in that area from the second century A.D. and the Peshitta Version was in use before the middle of the fifth century A.D. The Syriac Version of Ben Sira was produced during this period of time when writings sacred to the Jews were being put into the language of the people. This would have been done in the third or fourth century A.D.

The Syriac Version then underwent a Christian revision before the middle of the fifth century A.D. In this revision, a number of very important changes took place. These changes indicate a Christian hand at work:[8]

1. Passages contrary to belief in life after death are omitted;
2. passages implying creation of Wisdom (= Christ) are altered;
3. passages derogatory toward women or immodest are omitted or altered;
4. references to many of the great Jewish fathers are omitted; and,
5. passages extolling poverty are enhanced.

This Christian revision was completed before the middle of the fifth century A.D. and the exclusion of the Nestorians, since the manuscript tradition, both East and West, is so uniform.

---

[5] See Chapter 5, A.

[6] See Chapters 5, A.; 1, D.; and 2, A.

[7] See Chapter 2.

[8] See Chapter 5, A. M. Winter has argued that the Christian origin of the Syriac Ben Sira was very early (perhaps ca. 300 A.D., 1977: II, pp. 505-07). The original was an Ebionite version (1977: I, pp. 237-53), which was followed by an orthodox revision before the end of the fourth century A.D. (1977: II, pp. 494-507).

Bibliography

Adler, E. N.
1899–1900   Some missing Chapters of Ben Sira (7:20–12:1). *JQR* 12: 466–80.

Baars, Willem
1968   *New Syro-Hexaplaric Texts.* Leiden: Brill.

Baillet, M.
1956   Le travail d'edition des fragments manuscrits de Qumran. *RB* 63: 54.

Baillet, M., J. T. Milik, and R. deVaux
1962   Les "Petites Grottes" de Qumran. Discoveries in the Judaen Desert, III. Pp. 75–77. Oxford.

Barthelemy, D. and O. Rickenbacher
1973   *Konkordanz zum Hebräischen Sirach. Mit syrisch-hebräischen Index.* Göttingen: Vandenhoeck and Ruprecht.

Baumgarten, Joseph
1967–68   Some Notes on the Ben Sira Scroll From Masada. *JQR* 57–58: 323–27.

Baumstark, Anton
1922   *Geschichte der syrischen Literatur.* Bonn. Reprint, Berlin, 1968.
1935   Neue orientalische Probleme bibl. Textgeschichte. *ZDMG* XIV, N.F.: 80–118.

Baumstark, Anton and Adolf Rücker.
1964   Die Syrische Literatur. Pp. 168–204 in *Handbuch der Orientalistik,* Erste Abteilung *Der Nahe urd der Mittlere Osten,* Dritter Bank, *Semitistik.* Leiden: Brill.

Ben Yehuda, E.
1911–59   *A Complete Dictionary of Ancient and Modern Hebrew* (Hebrew). Jerusalem.

Biblia Sacra
1951   *Biblia Sacra. Juxta Versionem Simplicem quae dicitur Pschitta.* Tomus secundus. Beryti: Typis Typographiae Catholicae.

Bickell, G.
1882   Ein alphabetische Lied Jesus Sirach's. *ZKT* 6: 319–33.

Box, G. H. and W. O. E. Oesterley
    1913   Sirach. Pp. 268-517 in the *Apocrypha and Pseudepigrapha of
                    the Old Testament.* 1, ed. R. H. Charles. Oxford.

Brockelmann, Carl
    1895   Berlin *Lexicon Syriacum*
    1928   Halle, 2nd edition

Brown, F., S. R. Driver, and C. A. Briggs
    1959   *A Hebrew and English Dictionary.* Oxford.

Burkill, T. A.
    1962   Ecclesiasticus. Pp. 13-21 in *The Interpreters Dictionary of the
                    Bible,* 2, ed. G. A. Buttrick, et al. Nashville: Abingdon.

Burkitt, F. C.
    1904   *Early Eastern Christianity. St. Margaret's Lectures on the Syriac-
                    speaking Church.* London. John Murray.

Costaz, Louis
    1963   *Dictionnaire syriaque-français Syriac-English Dictionary.*
                    Beyrouth: Impr. catholique.

Cowley, A. E. and A. Neubauer
    1897   *The Original Hebrew of a Portion of Ecclesiasticus
                    (xxxix,15-xlix,11).* Oxford.
    1901   *Facsimiles of the Fragments Hitherto Recovered of the Book of
                    Ecclesiasticus in Hebrew.* Oxford and Cambridge.

DiLella, Alexander A.
    1962[1]   *A Text-Critical and Historical Study of the Hebrew Text of
                    Sirach.* Catholic University of America, Washington, DC
                    Dissertation.
    1962[2]   Qumran and the Geniza Fragments of Sirach. *CBQ* 24: 245-67.
    1963   Authenticity of the Geniza Fragments of Sirach. *Bib* 44: 171-200.
    1964   The Recently Identified Leaves of Sirach in Hebrew. *Bib* 45:
                    153-67.
    1966   *The Hebrew Text of Sirach. A Text-critical and Historical Study.*
                    Studies in Classical Literature, 1. The Hague: Mouton and Co.

Dirksen, P. B.
    1972   *The Transmission of the Text in the Peshitta manuscripts of the
                    Book of Judges.* Leiden: Brill.

Duensing, H.
    1906   *Christlich-palästinisch-aramäische Texte und Fragmente.*
                    Göttingen.

Duesberg, Hilaire and Paul Auvray
    1953   *Le Livre de L'Ecclésiastique La Sainte Bible de l'École Biblique
                    de Jérusalem.* Paris: Les Éditions du Cerf.

Eck, Werner
1969   Die Eroberung von Massada und eine neue Inschrift des L.
        Flavius Silva Nonnius Bassus. *ZNW* 60: 282–89.

Eissfeldt, Otto
1965   *The Old Testament. An Introduction.* New York: Harper and
        Row.

Elliger, K. and W. Rudolph
1976/77 *Biblia Hebraica Stuttgartensia.* Stuttgart: Deutsche Bibelstitung.

Eusebius Pamphili.
1953   *Ecclesiastical History* I.13.1–9. New York: Fathers of the
        Church, Inc.

Forster, A. H.
1959   The Date of Ecclesticus. *ATR* 41: 1–9.

Fox, Douglas J.
        The "Matthew-Luke Commentary" of Philoxenus. Missoula,
        MT: Scholars Press.

Gaster, M.
1899–1900 A New Fragment of Ben Sira (chapters 18, 19, and 20) JQR 12:
        688–702.

Ginsberg, H. L.
1955   The Original Hebrew of Ben Sira 12:10–14. *JBL* 74: 93–95.

Ginzberg, L.
1906   Randglossen zum hebräischen Ben Sira. Pp. 609–25 in *Orien-
        talische Studien T. Nöldeke*, II. Giessen.

Goodspeed, E. J.
1939   *The Story of the Apocrypha.* Chicago: University of Chicago
        Press.

Goodspeed, E. J. (trans)
1959   *The Apocrypha.* New York.

Goshen-Gottstein, M.
1964   The Edition of the Syro-hexapla Materials. *Textus* IV: 230–231.
1970   *A Syriac-English Glossary with Etymological Notes.* Based on
        Brockelmann's *Syriac Chrestomathy.* Wiesbaden: Otto
        Harrassowitz.

Gwynn, John
1887   Paulus Tellensis. Pp. 266–71 in *A Dictionary of Christian
        Biography* IV, eds. William Smith and Henry Wace. London:
        John Murray.

Hadas, M.
1959   *The Apocrypha.* Trans. by E. J. Goodspeed. New York.

Hart, J. H. A.
1909   *Ecclesiasticus. The Greek Text of Codex 248.* Edited with a textual commentary and prolegomena. Cambridge.

Hartman, Louis F.
1961   Sirach in Hebrew and Greek. *CBQ* 23: 443–51.

Hatch, E. and H. A. Redpath
1906   *A Concordance to the Septuagint, Supplement: Deutero-Canonical Books,* by H. A. Redpath. Oxford.

Historical Dictionary
1973   *The Book of Ben Sira. Text, Concordance and an Analysis of the Vocabulary. The Historical Dictionary of the Hebrew Language.* Jerusalem: The Academy of the Hebrew Language and the Shrine of the Book.

Holladay, William L. (ed.)
1971   *A Concise Hebrew and Aramaic Lexicon of the Old Testament.* Grand Rapids: Eerdmans.

Jastrow, M.
1950[1]   *A Dictionary of the Targumim.*
1950[2]   *The Talmud Babli and Yerushalmi, and the Midrashic Literature,* 1–2 London-New York, 1903. Reprint, New York: Pardes, 1950.

Jean, C. F. and J. Hoftijzer
1965   Dictionnaire des Inscriptions sémitiques de L'Ouest. Leiden: Brill.

Jellicoe, Sidney
1968   *The Septuagint and Modern Study.* Oxford: Clarendon Press.

Josephus
1943   Pp. 732–36 in *Josephus VII Jewish Antiquities* XII-XIV, R. Marcus. *Loeb Classical Library.* Harvard.

Katz, Saul
1892   *Die Scholien des Gregorius Abulfaragius Bar Hebraeus zum Weisheitsbuch des Joshua ben Sira nach vier Handschriften des Horreum mysteriorum.* Frankfurt.

Kahle, Paul E.
1959   *The Cairo Geniza.* 2d ed. New York: Fredrick Praeger.

Kearns, C.
1969   Ecclesiasticus, or the Wisdom of Jesus the Son of Sirach. Pp. 541–51 of *A New Catholic Commentary on Holy Scripture,* eds. R. Fuller, L. Johnston, C. Kearns. London: Thomas Nelson and Sons.

Kelley, J. N. D.
1960   *Early Christian Doctrines.* New York: Harper and Row.

Koehler, L. and W. Baumgartner
1958   *Lexicon in veteris testamenti libros,* with *Supplement.* Leiden: Brill.

Kuhn, K. G. (ed.)
1960   *Konkordanz zu den Qumrantexten.* Göttingen: Vandenhoeck und Ruprecht.
1963   Nachträge zur "Konkordanz zu den Qumrantexten." *RQ* IV: 163–234.

Lagrange, J.
1925   L origine de la version syro-palestinienne des évangiles. *RB* 34: 481–504.

Lake, Kirsopp
1928   *The Text of the New Testament.* 6th ed. London.

Lévi, Israel
1898   *L'Ecclésiastique ou La Sagesse de Jésus, Fils de Sira.* Première Partie (xxxix,15 à xlix,11). Paris: Ernest Leroux.
1900   Fragments de deux nouveax manuscrits hebreux de l'Ecclesiastique. *REJ* 40: 1–30.
1901   L'Ecclesiastique. Deuxième Partie (Varia). Paris: E. Leroux.
1902   Quelques citations de l'Ecclésiastique. *REJ* 1902: 291–94.
1904   *The Hebrew Text of the Book of Ecclesiasticus.* Leiden: Brill.
1932   Un nouveau fragment de Ben Sira. *REJ* 92: 136–45.

Liddell, H. G., R. Scott, H. S. Jones, and R. McKenzie
1968   *A Greek-English Lexicon.* 9th ed. (1940) with Supplement (1968). Oxford: Clarendon Press.

Lisowsky, G.
1958   *Konkordanz zum hebräischen Alten Testament.* 2d ed. Stuttgart: Württembergische Bibelanstalt.

LIST
1961   *List of Old Testament Peshitta Manuscripts,* ed. Peshitta Institute Leiden University. Leiden: Brill. See also Peshitta Institute Communications.

Lohse, E. (ed.)
1964   *Die Texte aus Qumran. Hebräisch und deutsch.* Munich: Kösel-Verlag.

Mandelkern, Solomon
1967   *Veteris Testamenti Concordantiae hebraicae atque chaldaicae.* 7th ed. Tel Aviv: Shocken.

Marcus, J.
1931   *The Newly Discovered Original Hebrew of Ben Sira (Ecclesiasticus xxxii.16-xxxiv.1): The Fifth Manuscript and a Prosodic Version of Ben Sira (Ecclesiasticus xxii.22-xxiii.9).* Philadelphia.
1930-31   A Fifth Manuscript of Ben Sira, with Corrections. *JQR* n.s. 21: 223-40.

Margoliouth, G.
1899-1900   The Original Hebrew of Ecclesiasticus xxxi.12-31 and xxxvi.22-xxxvii.26. *JQR* 12: 1-33.

McCullough, W. Stuart
1982   *A Short History of Syriac Christianity to the Rise of Islam.* Chico, CA: Scholars Press.

McHardy, W. D.
1945-48   Ben-Ze'eb's Edition of the Peshitta Text of Ecclesiasticus. *ZAW* 61: 193-94.

McKeating, H.
1973   Jesus ben Sira's Attitude to Women. *Expository Times* 85:191ff.

Metzger, Bruce M.
1962   Syriac Versions. Pp. 754-55 in vol. IV of *The Interpreter's Dictionary of the Bible,* ed. George A. Buttrick. New York: Abingdon.
1977   *The Early Versions of the New Testament. Their Origin, Transmission, and Limitations.* Oxford: Clarendon Press.

Middendorp, Th.
1973   *Die Stellung Jesu Ben Siras zwischen Judentum und Hellenismus.* Leiden: Brill.

Milik, J. T.
1966   *Un fragment mal placé dans l'édition du Siracide de Masada. Bib* 47: 425ff.

Moss, Cyril
1962   *Cataloque of Syriac Printed Books and Related Literature in the British Museum.* London: The Trustees of the British Museum.

Nebe, G. W.
1970   Sirach 42:5c *ZAW* 82, no. 2: 283-86.

Nestle, E.
1902   Syriac Versions. P. 652 in Vol. 4 of *Hastings Dictionary of the Bible,* ed. J. Hastings. Edinburgh: T. & T. Clark.
1923   Sirach (Book of). P. 548 in vol. 4 of *A Dictionary of the Bible,* ed. J. Hastings. New York: Scribners.

Neusner, Jacob
1964   The Conversion of Adiabene to Judaism: A New Perspective.
        JBL 83: 60–66.

Oesterley, W. O. E.
1935   *An Introduction to the Books of the Apocrypha.* New York:
        Macmillan.

Penar, Tadeusz
1975   *Northwest Semitic Philology and the Hebrew Fragments of Ben
        Sira.* Biblica et Orientalia n. 28. Rome: Biblical Institute Press.
1976   Three Philological Notes on the Hebrew Fragments of Ben Sira.
        Bib 57: 112–13.

Peshitta Institute Communications
1962   *VT* 12: 127f, 237f, 351.
1963   *VT* 13: 349.
1977   *VT* 27: 508–11.

Peters, N.
1902   *Der jüngst wiederaufgefundene hebräische Text des Buches
        Ecclesiasticus. Untersucht herausgegeben, übersetzt und mit
        Kritischen Noten versehen.* Freiburg in Breisgau.

Phillips, G. (ed.)
1876   *Doctrine of Addai.* London. New edition forthcoming from
        Scholars Press, 1981, ed. by George Howard.

Rabinowitz, Isaac
1971   The Qumran Hebrew Original of Ben Sira's Concluding Acrostic
        on Wisdom. *HUCA* XLII: 173–84.

Roberts, Bleddyn J.
1951   *The Old Testament Text and Versions. The Hebrew Text in
        Transmission and the History of the Ancient Versions.* Cardiff:
        University of Wales Press.

Rüger, Hans Peter
1970[1] *Text und Textform in hebräischen Sirach.* Beihefte zur Zeitschrift
        für die alttestamentliche Wissenschaft 112, ed. Georg Fohrer.
        Berlin: Walter de Gruyter & Co.
1970[2] Zum Text von Sir 40:10 und Ex 10:21. *ZAW* 80, no. 1: 103–09.

Sanders, J. A.
1965   *The Psalms Scroll of Qumran Cave II. Discoveries in the
        Judaean Desert IV.* Pp. 79–85. Oxford. Cf. M. Delcor, *Textus* 6
        (1968), pp. 27–47 for corrections.

Schechter, S.
1896   A Fragment of the Original Text of Ecclesiasticus (39:15–40:7).
        Expositor, Fifth series, 4: 1–15.

1897-98   Genizah Specimens. Ecclesiasticus. *JQR* 10: 197-206.
1899-1900 A Further Fragment of Ben Sira (Ms C: chapters 4,5,25,26). *JQR* 12: 456-65.

Schechter, S. and C. Taylor
1899   *The Wisdom of Ben Sira: Portions of the Book Ecclesiasticus from Hebrew Manuscripts in the Cairo Genizeh Collection Presented to the University of Cambridge.* Cambridge.

Schirmann, J.
1957-58   *Dap ḥadaš mittok seper ben-Sira' ha-'ibri. Tarbiz* 27: 440-43.
1960   *Dappim nos pim mittok seper Ben Sira'. Tarbiz* 29: 125-34.

Schoeps, Hans-Joachim
1969   *Jewish Christianity. Factional Disputes in the Early Church.* Trans. Douglas R. A. Hare. Philadelphia: Fortress.

Schulthess, Fr.
1905   *Christlich-Palästinische Fragment aus der Omajjaden-Moschee zu Damascus.* Abh. d. Kgl. Ges. d. Wiss. zu Göttingen. Philol.-hist. Kl. N. F. VIII 3. Berlin.

Segal, J. B.
1970   *Edessa "the Blessed City."* Oxford: Clarendon.

Segal, M. H.
1934   The Evolution of the Hebrew Text of Ben Sira. *JQR* n.s. 25: 91-149.
1958   *Seper ben-Sira' ha-šalem.* 2d ed. Jerusalem. Includes the 1957-58 Schirmann publication.
1964   Ben Sira in Qumran. *Tarbiz* 33: 243ff.

Skehan, P. W.
1968   Sirach 40:11-17. *CBQ* 30: 570-72.
1966   Review of Y. Yadin, *The Ben Sira Scroll from Masada* (1965). *JBL* 85: 260-62.
1971[1]   The Acrostic Poem in Sirach 51:13-30. *HTR* 64: 387-400.
1971[2]   Staves, and Nails, and Scribal Slips (Ben Sira 44:2-5). *BASOR* 200: 66-71.
1976   Ecclesiasticus. Pp. 250-251 in *Supplementary Volume* of the *Interpreter's Dictionary of the Bible,* ed. K. Crim, et al. Nashville: Abingdon.

Smend, Rudolf
1906[1]   *Die Weisheit des Jesus Sirach. Hebräisch und Deutsch. Mit einem hebräischen Glossar.* Berlin: Georg Reimer.
1906[2]   *Die Weisheit des Jesus Sirach. Erklärt.* Berlin: Georg Reimer.
1907[1]   *Griechisch-syrisch-hebräischer Index zur Weisheit des Jesus Sirach.* Berlin: Georg Reimer.

1907²   Nachträgliches zur Textüberlieferung des syrischen Sirach. *ZAW* 27: 271–75.

Smith, J. Payne
1903   *A Compendius Syriac Dictionary.* Oxford.

Smith, R. Payne, et al. (eds.)
1897, 1901   *Thesaurus syriarus.* 1–2. Oxford.

Snaith, John G.
1974   *Ecclesiasticus.* The Cambridge Bible Commentary, eds. P. R. Ackroyd, A. R. C. Leaney, and J. W. Packer. Cambridge University Press.

Stevenson, J. (ed.)
1965   *A New Eusebius. Documents illustrative of the history of the Church to A.D. 337.* London: SPCK.

Strack, H. L.
1903   *Die Spruche Jesuś, des Sohnes Sirach.* Leipzig.

Strugnell, J.
1969/70   Notes and Queries on the Ben Sira Scroll from Masada. *Eretz Israel* IX: 109–19.

Swete, H. B.
1907   *The Old Testament in Greek,* vol. 2. 3d ed. Cambridge.

Torrey, C. C.
1945   *The Aprocryphal Literature.* New Haven: Yale University Press.
1950   The Hebrew of the Genizeh Sirach. Pp. 585–602 in *Alexander Marx Jubilee Volume,* ed. S. Liebermann. New York: The Jewish Theological Seminary of America.

Van Puyvelde, Cl.
N.D.   Versions syriques. Pp. 834–83 in vol. VIII of *Dictionnaire de la Bible, Supplement.* Paris.

Vattioni, Francesco
1968   *Ecclesiastico: Ebraico, Graeca, Latina, Siriaca.* Napoli: Institute Orientale Di Napoli.

deVaux, R.
1950   A propos des manuscrits de la Mer Morte. *RB* 57: 417–29.

Vawter, Bruce
1972   Intimations of Immortality in the Old Testament. *JBL* 91: 158–71.

Vööbus, A.
1954   *Early Versions of the New Testament. Manuscript Studies. Papers of the Estonia Theological Society in Exile, 6.* Stockholm.

1970   *Discoveries of Very Important Manuscript Sources for the Syro-Hexapla. Contributions to the Research on the Septuagint. Papers of the Estonian Theological Society in Exile, 20.* Stockholm.

1971   *The Hexapla and the Syro-Hexapla. Very Important Discoveries for Septuagint Research. Papers of the Estonian Theological Faculty in Exile, 22.* Stockholm.

1976   Syriac Versions. Pp. 848–54 in *Supplementary Volume,* ed. Keith Krim of *The Interpreter's Dictionary of the Bible.* Nashville: Abingdon.

Winter, Michael M.

1976   *A Concordance to the Peshitta Version of Ben Sira.* Leiden: Brill.

1977[1]   The Origins of Ben Sira in Syriac (Part I). Peshitta Institute Communication XII. *VT* XXVII, fasc. 2: 237–53.

1977[2]   The Origins of Ben Sira in Syriac (Part II). Peshitta Institute Communication XIII. *VT* XVII, fasc. 4: 494–507.

Wolfson, H. A.

1970   *The Philosophy of the Church Fathers. Vol. I: Faith, Trinity, Incarnation.* 3d ed. Cambridge: Harvard University Press.

Würthwein, Ernst

1973   *Der Text Des Alten Testaments. Eine Einführung in Die Biblia Hebraica.* 4th ed. Württembergische Bibelanstalt Stuttgart.

Yadin, Yigael

1965[1]   The Ben Sira Scroll from Masada. *Eretz Israel* 8 (E. L. Sukenik Memorial Volume). Jerusalem.

1965[2]   *The Ben Sira Scroll from Masada.* Jerusalem: The Israel Exploration Society and the Shrine of the Book.

Ziegler, Joseph

1959   Hat Lukian der griechischen Sirach rezendiert? *Bib* 40: 210–29.

1965   *Sapientia Iesu Filii Sirach. Septuaginta. Vetus Testamentum Graecum Auctoritate Societatis Litterarum Gottingensis editum.* XII,2, Göttingen: Vandenhoeck and Ruprecht.